Thoughtful ministers, students, and laypersons will find in *After Fundamentalism* a readable and helpful paradigm that invites evangelicals to be fully children of the twentieth century, reasonably and with integrity — while, at the same time, maintaining the historic substance of Christianity and holding to an evangelical faith.

Bernard L. Ramm, Ph.D., is Professor of Theology at the American Baptist Seminary of the West in Berkeley, California. A noted scholar, Dr. Ramm is the author of numerous books, including *Handbook of Contemporary Theology, The God Who Makes a Difference, Protestant Biblical Interpretation*, and *Varieties of Christian Apologetics*.

AFTER
FUNDAMENTALISM

AFTER FUNDAMENTALISM

The Future of Evangelical Theology

Bernard Ramm

1817

HARPER & ROW, PUBLISHERS, SAN FRANCISCO

Cambridge, Hagerstown, New York, Philadelphia
London, Mexico City, São Paulo, Sydney

FIRST EDITION

Designed by Donna Davis

Library of Congress Cataloging in Publication Data

Ramm, Bernard L., 1916–
    AFTER FUNDAMENTALISM.

  Bibliography: p. 211
  Includes index.
    1. Theology—Methodology.   2. Evangelicalism.
3. Enlightenment.   4. Barth, Karl, 1886–1968.
5. Modernist-fundamentalist controversy.   I. Title.
BR118.R33   1982   230'.044   82-47792
  ISBN 0–06–066789–3

83 84 85 86 87 10 9 8 7 6 5 4 3 2 1

Contents

Preface

This book has a very narrow compass. It is not a survey of Barthian theology. Nor does it intend to be a complete survey of Barth's thought on any given topic. It is an essay in theological methodology.

The leading themes are as follows: (1) The Enlightenment was a shattering experience for orthodox theology from which it has never fully recovered. (2) Neither religious liberalism nor orthodoxy had the right strategy for interacting with the Enlightenment with reference to the continuing task of Christian theology. (3) Of all the efforts of theologians to come to terms with the Enlightenment, Karl Barth's theology has been the most thorough. (4) He thereby offers to evangelical theology a paradigm of how best to come to terms with the Enlightenment.

My basic methodology is to first review the impact of the Enlightenment on a given doctrine. Then I review how Barth handles the doctrine in view of the criticism of the Enlightenment. Finally, I show how Barth's stance may be a paradigm for evangelical theology (even if only in a heuristic sense). By *paradigm* I mean a model, a pattern or schema, for writing theology. By *heuristic* I mean a hypothesis which may not prove to be true but which is instrumental in leading to the discovery of the true one.

The fine *Letters: 1922–1966** was published too late to be included in the exposition of this book, but it alters nothing I have written and would have served only to reinforce documentation.

---

* *Correspondence of Karl Barth and Rudolph Bultmann,* trans. and ed. by Goeffrey W. Bromiley; ed. by Bernd Jaspert (Grand Rapids: Wm. B. Eerdmans, 1981).

Barth's Definition of Theology

Of all the sciences which stir the head and heart, theology is the fairest. It is closest to human reality and gives us the clearest view of the truth after which all science quests. It best illustrates the time-honored and profound word: "Fakultät." It is a landscape, like the landscape of Umbria or Tuscany, in which distant perspectives are always clear. Theology is a masterpiece, as well-planned and yet as bizarre as the cathedrals of Cologne and Milan. What a miserable lot of theologians—and what miserable periods there have been in the history of theology— when they have not realized this!

At this point we may refer to the fact that if its task is correctly seen and grasped, theology as a whole, in its parts and in their interconnexion, in its content and method, is, apart from anything else, a peculiarly beautiful science. Indeed, we can confidently say that it is the most beautiful of all the sciences. To find the sciences distasteful is the mark of the Philistine. It is an extreme form of Philistinism to find, or to be able to find, theology distasteful. The theologian who has no joy in his work is not a theologian at all. Sulky faces, morose thoughts and boring ways of speaking are intolerable in this science. May God deliver us from what the Catholic Church reckons one of the seven sins of the monk—*taedium*—in respect of the great spiritual truths with which theology has to do. But we must know, of course, that it is only God who can keep us from it.

Barth in a Nutshell

Idealist, then Christian Socialist, Kierkegaardian, Heideggerian, then fed by the great springs of the Reformation and of the church fathers, close to the texts of the sixteenth century to contemporize them, as of those of the nineteenth century to understand and criticize them, enlarging his biblical exegesis as well as his commentaries on Kant, Descartes, Leibniz, and Schopenhauer, Barth seems to have apprehended a world becoming more and more vast without his criticisms ever losing their pungency nor his research his concentration.

ANDRÉ DUMAS

1

The Quest

I HAD JUST FINISHED a lecture on my version of American evangelical theology. When I was asked by a shrewd listener to define American evangelical theology more precisely, I experienced inward panic. Like a drowning man who sees parts of his life pass before him at great speed (an experience I have had), so my theology passed before my eyes. I saw my theology as a series of doctrines picked up here and there, like a rag-bag collection. To stutter out a reply to that question was one of the most difficult things I have ever had to do on a public platform.

The experience set me to reflection. Why was my theology in the shape it was? The answer that kept coming back again and again was that theologically I was the product of the orthodox-liberal debate that has gone on for a century. It is a debate that has warped evangelical theology. The controversial doctrines have been given far more importance than they deserve in a good theological system. Other important doctrines have been neglected. The result of that debate has been to shape evangelical theology into the form of haphazardly related doctrines. I did not have a theology whose methodology was scientifically ascertained, nor doctrines scientifically interrelated nor properly defended. That is why I could not give a reasonable account of my theology when asked to do so.

———————⊷———————

As I sought to reground my theology, I looked around for some new option. One option was to pick up one of the great theological systems of the past, but none glowed with such a luminous light as to attract me. In view of our current knowledge of Holy Scripture and other progress in learning, all these systems represented a premature foreclosure on the biblical materials. Another option was to latch on to one of the current theologies I touched on as in my annual lecturing I reviewed contemporary theology. But there was a measure of novelty about each of them that warned me that they did not have enduring substance.

However, in my reading it became more and more apparent that one of the great cultural watersheds of the history of human culture was the Enlightenment. One cannot explain the great Schleiermacher, for example, without first explaining the Enlightenment. One cannot explain the modern mind at all without spending much time in the eighteenth-century developments, the century of the Enlightenment. It finally became apparent to me that the place to begin my quest was with the investigation of the Enlightenment.

I set myself to the task of informing myself in great detail about the Enlightenment—*Aufklärung, L'Illumination.* In short definition, the Enlightenment was the cultural epoch that prevailed in Europe in the eighteenth century although it had its pre-history and in many ways continues today.

The Enlightenment was a period of great diversity. It had a different character in each country, and within each country there was a diversity of opinion on politics, religion, and philosophy. For a good history of the period, see *The Enlightenment in National Context* (edited by Roy Porter and Mikuláš Teich), which has chapters on the Enlightenment in England, Scotland, France, the Netherlands, Switzerland, Italy, Protestant Germany, Catholic Germany, Austria, Bohemia, Sweden, Russia, and America.

One way to understand the mood of the Enlightenment is to list those words and concepts that were given great approval and those which were regarded with distrust. The approved concepts were *reason, freedom, nature, utility, happiness, rights, tolerance, deism, rational Christianity, natural religion, social contract, science, autonomy, harmony, and optimism.* The disapproved concepts were *authority, antiquity, tradition, church, revelation,* the *supernatural,* and *theological explanations.* The value placed on these terms will become clear in the following discussion.

The Enlightenment was the period when the radical secularization of European culture began. In place of the state as a divine institution paralleling the church (as historically taught by both Roman Catholic and Protestant theologians), the "enlightened" state was now to be theoretically grounded in some version of the social contract. The social contract theory of the state argued that a government was a mutual arrangement among its citizens (which could take many forms), not a divine institution. Education began to be more and more grounded on humanistic presuppositions and less and less on Christian and classical presuppositions. The schoolteacher became more important in the community than the pastor. Along with the Industrial Revolution, the Enlightenment helped mold the vast secular populations that today characterize all the big industrial cities of the world. It started a decline in church attendance that in the latter part of this century has become endemic, giving especially Europe the appearance of a religious territory long ago burned out.

Peter Gay, an accomplished student of the Enlightenment, calls the mentality that emerged from the Enlightenment "modern paganism." This character is seen clearly in university education today. Education in the Middle Ages and at the time of the Reformation was based on Christian presuppositions, Christian revelation, Christian theology. Modern universities are based on the modern paganism (sometimes disguised by the more tempered word *humanism*) that emerged from the Enlightenment.

In the Enlightenment, the scholars, the intelligentsia, the literati (*les philosophes,* as the French called them, or the *eggheads,* in recent jargon), gave up orthodox Christianity. No longer were the great Christian presuppositions considered the basis of European civilization, culture, education, law, or government.

Historian Henry F. May has written that only Christians are still worried about the Enlightenment.[1] That is right: The Enlightenment sent shock waves through Christian theology as nothing did before or after. Theology has never been the same since the Enlightenment. And therefore each and every theology, evangelical included, must assess its relationship to the Enlightenment.

————— ∞ —————

A number of ideas that characterized the Enlightenment died out because they were too narrow or too provincial or simply because they were wrong, such as the simplistic definition of Reason. But among the numerous movements, philosophies, affectations, and ideologies, certain ideas did not die out. On the contrary, they persist down to the present time and form part of what we may call "the modern mentality." Many of these ideas are discussed in detail later; here I list them without comment.

1. The beginnings of scientific history
2. The contention that whatever is claimed as truth must justify itself before the bar of reason
3. The primacy of nature as the source for answers to fundamental human questions
4. The necessity for literary and historical criticism of all documents of the past—secular, ecclesiastical, and biblical
5. The need for freedom to advance progress and human welfare
6. The need for a critical philosophy
7. The belief that ethics is autonomous and not dependent on religion or theology
8. The fundamental suspicion of all truth claims grounded in authority, tradition, or divine revelation

9. The high evaluation of the sciences and the virtue of progress in scientific knowledge
10. The affirmation that tolerance is the supreme disposition in matters of religion
11. The need to continue the humanism that first broke through into Western consciousness in the time of the Renaissance

The following movement in history was known as the Counter-Enlightenment. It was a period in which the extremes of the Enlightenment were corrected and neglected aspects of human experience were introduced into the discussion (for example, the romantic). Romantics were those people who looked at nature, humanity, history, spirit, and God in depth. Religion to them was more of the nature of intuition and feeling than a rational reception of dogma. Our concern is with those elements of the Enlightenment that lived beyond the Counter-Enlightenment and still continue to shape modern mentality.

Ernst Troeltsch was an unusual scholar in the breadth of his learning, which encompassed theology, philosophy, church history, and historical science. It was his judgment that the Enlightenment was the crucial century in which modern mentality was shaped. Heribert Raab said that the Enlightenment was the most revolutionary age in all human history.[2] Other specialists of the Enlightenment—such as Wilhem Anz, Franz Schümmer, Paul Tillich, and James Livingston—claim that all our modern problems in philosophy and theology were born in the period of the Enlightenment and that we are still working on their solutions. In this work, I mean by the term *Enlightenment* that particular part of the Enlightenment that has endured and continues to shape modern mentality. This part of the Enlightenment is critical for the formulation of theology in the twentieth century.

In my reading on the Enlightenment, I found out that I had to correct a view of the history of theology that I had previously held. I thought that orthodoxy, with its view of theology and Scripture, had prevailed until the time of Friedrich Schleiermacher. I thought it was Schleiermacher and the various versions of liberal Christianity after him that had upset Protestant orthodox theology. On the contrary, I found out that it was the Neologians or Innovators who had accomplished this in the eighteenth century (for example, Johann Michaelis, Johann Jerusalem, Johann Döderlein, Johann Semler, Johann Spalding, and Jacob Baumgarten). These men are unknown in the United States except to specialists in the history of theology, and that is why I had never encountered them before. It was either the Neologian Karl Bahrdt or Johann Semler who first used the expression "liberal theology."

The Neologians, in their work in biblical criticism, upset the orthodox doctrine of inspiration as set out in the seventeenth century. They made a concerted attack on orthodoxy in general and on Lutheran orthodoxy in particular. They made a strong, systematic protest against the supernatural in historic Christianity. And they attacked such particular doctrines as eternal judgment, the existence of the devil, the trinity, the vicarious atonement, the deity of Christ, the virgin birth, the bodily resurrection of Christ, Chalcedonian Christology, and Lutheran Christology. Chalcedonian Christology is that Christology associated with the famous Definition of Chalcedon (451) in which it was affirmed that Jesus Christ had both a divine and a human nature united in one person. Lutheran Christology was a special effort to spell out the manner in which the human and divine natures coalesced in the incarnation. That which was started by the Neologians in the middle of the eighteenth century was more thoroughly carried out by the rationalists who prevailed in the latter part of the century.

This is why the Enlightenment began to worry me, and why it ought to worry all evangelical theologians.

It is generally agreed that the founder of liberal Christianity was Friedrich Daniel Ernst Schleiermacher (1768–1834), who has also been called the greatest theologian between Calvin and Barth. It is therefore important to inspect his thought and see how he reacted to the Enlightenment.

Schleiermacher began his education among the Moravians. They were noted for their Pietism in their spiritual life, but as far as they were concerned with theology they were very close to traditional Lutheran theology. While Schleiermacher was studying under the Moravians at Barby, he encountered the Neologians of the Enlightenment and was deeply impressed by them. He found himself in such disagreement with the theological emphases of the Moravians that he left their school at Barby and transferred to the University of Halle, which had Neologians on its faculty. Barth claims that Schleiermacher accepted the Neologians' criticism of orthodox Lutheran dogma.[3]

As much as Schleiermacher agreed with the criticism of orthodox theology that was so characteristic of the Englightenment, he did not approve of its positive program in religion. The rut was too narrow, and the religion too rationalistic and moralistic. He announced the outlines of his own creative synthesis in his book *On Religion: Speeches to Its Cultured Despisers* (1799), a book Barth himself said that we cannot read too many times.

Schleiermacher's grand synthesis may be summarized as follows: (1) The Enlightenment criticism of orthodoxy is right. The days of an inerrant Scripture and Lutheran orthodox dogmatic theology are over. (2) German romantic idealistic philosophy offers a far richer ground for Christian faith and theology than does the moralistic, rationalistic religion of the Enlightenment. (3) The whole range of Christian theology can be reinterpreted on the basis of this kind of philosophy, and we can be both modern and Christians.

The book was aimed at the cultured (educated) despisers of Christianity who had come to that attitude in their thinking via the developments of the Enlightenment. Schleiermacher felt that if they could see that the Christian faith was deeply cultural, deeply human, really universal, they would return to it.

The title of Christof Senf's book plots the position of Schleiermacher's theology: *Wahrhaftigkeit und Wahrheit: Die Theologie zwischen Orthodoxie und Aufklärung* ("Truthfulness and Truth: Theology Between Orthodoxy and Enlightenment"). It is a theology that disagrees with orthodoxy and with the religion of the Enlightenment. At the same, it agrees with the Enlightenment's criticism of orthodox theology. It therefore lies between (*zwischen*) orthodoxy and the Enlightenment.

Let us look more closely at at Schleiermacher, the Enlightenment, Christianity, and his new synthesis. First of all, Schleiermacher agrees with the Enlightenment criticism of orthodoxy. That version of Christianity has run its course. Modern learning makes it an impossible option. On the other hand, the religion of the Enlightenment period is also to be criticized. The theology of deism and the religious philosophy of Kant both distorted the nature of true religion. They made too easy an identification of morality with religion. Schleiermacher is a romantic, and therefore he defends a romantic interpretation of religion and Christianity and so forms the grand new synthesis we call liberal Christianity.

This is precisely how Paul Tillich sets out the theology of Schleiermacher (*A History of Christian Thought* and *Perspectives on Nineteenth and Twentieth Century Theology*). He sees Schleiermacher and Hegel faced with the same problem: how can we be modern and Christian at the same time? The answer was to go beyond the rationalism and deism of the Enlightenment to the new synthesis of modern learning, modern philosophy, and the reinterpretation of historic Christian dogma. In passing, Tillich says that this is his way, too, for it is the only viable option for the twentieth century.

If the Enlightenment collapsed orthodoxy as an option for Europe's intelligentsia, and if liberal Christianity was born as a reaction to the Enlightenment, it seems obvious to me that evangelical theology must come to its terms with the Enlightenment.

I must now pick up another thread in my theological trek. In the middle of the 1940s, I chanced on a copy of Barth's *Church Dogmatics* (I/1). At that time Volume I/1 was the only volume in English. On the one hand, the volume frustrated me. It contained so many untranslated citations in Latin and

Greek—so unrealistic for American readers. It contained long technical sections in fine print. And I was confused by the novel meanings given to traditional theological concepts. On the other hand, I sensed that something important was being said. It was certainly not a rehash of older liberal theology. And it was strangely different from the standard orthodox authors I had read.

At this time I was just starting graduate studies in philosophy, which were to consume my academic energies for the next five years. So my reading of Barth was aborted. Nevertheless, I kept hearing about Barth—a book review, a conversation, remarks in a theological article, a comment in a lecture. I began to come across statements to the effect that here was a theologian of the same stature as Augustine, Thomas, Luther, Calvin, and Schleiermacher. That stimulated my imagination.

It just so happened that when I started to systematically read Barth, I also began to study and assimilate the writings of Abraham Kuyper, especially *Principles of Sacred Theology*. Although the lives of the two men overlapped, Kuyper died more than a decade before the first volume of Barth's *Church Dogmatics* was published. Kuyper was far more profound, far more philosophically minded, far more culturally oriented than the orthodox authors I had read. Time and time again I found parallels between Barth's thought and Kuyper's. Kuyper's view on inspiration and revelation were far more profound and enlightened than any I had read heretofore, and his concept of theology was the first truly sophisticated one I had read. In this way Kuyper provided a small but important bridge to Barth.

Also influential at this time was my reading of P. T. Forsyth, *The Principle of Authority*. From Forsyth, I learned that the *content* of Scripture had as much to do with its authority as the formal claims of revelation and inspiration. I had been taught that one proceeds from revelation to inspiration to the theological content of Scripture. Forsyth showed how artificial that sequence was. One comes to Christianity through the person of Christ and his Gospel—the content. This idea prepared me for Barth's major contention that only the content of the Christian faith sells the faith to us; nothing else can.

When the chance came for me to study in Europe for an academic year, there was no question in my mind but that the place to go was Basel, where Barth was still alive and teaching. That was the year 1957–58. The inspiration had finally come to me that of all the contemporary theologians the one who was doing the best job of relating historic Reformed theology to the Enlightenment was Karl Barth. Hence my quest for a viable evangelical theology, my sense of the importance of the Enlightenment for theology, and the theology of Karl Barth intersected. That is the theme of the next section.

However, I must comment at this point on two books. Donald Bloesch has a chapter on Barth and the Enlightenment in his book *Jesus Is Victor: Karl Barth's Doctrine of Salvation* (Chap. 6). I had a rough draft of this manuscript done before I read that chapter. However, my treatment of Barth and the Enlightenment is very different from Bloesch's. This was also the case with Gregory G. Bolich's book *Karl Barth and Evangelicalism*. Our theses do overlap, but again my treatment of Barth and evangelicalism is different from Bolich's. I present Barth's theological methodology systematically, as a viable option for the future of evangelical theology, and illustrate the thesis by examining Barth's methodology at a number of key doctrines.

Notes

1. Henry F. May, *The Enlightenment in America* (New York: Oxford University Press, 1976), p. xvii.
2. Heribert Raab, "Enlightenment," *Sacramentum Mundi* 2, pp. 230–232.
3. Karl Barth, *Protestant Theology in the Nineteenth Century*, trans. B. Cozens and H. H. Hartwell (Valley Forge, Pa.: Judson Press, 1968), p. 168.

2

My Problem

By READING BARTH'S *Church Dogmatics* systematically every day according to a set schedule, I got beyond the Barth of the theological clichés, of the superficial generalizations, of the evangelical caricatures, and of the sanitary summaries of his theology in surveys of contemporary theology. I got to Barth the man, who walks through the thousands of pages of his theology. But I found a strange man, and a problem.

I found a man universally respected. He was honored in such great theological centers as Rome, Geneva, Paris, Copenhagen, Edinburgh, Princeton, and Chicago. At the time of his retirement, he had a chest full of eleven doctor's robes from the honorary degrees given to him by great universities. While yet alive, he was compared to Augustine, Thomas, Luther, Calvin, and Schleiermacher.

On reading him, I did not find him quite the kind of man that modern theologians would so honor. His theology has its own twists and turns, but I found him defending the ancient Christology of the church fathers as well as their doctrine of the trinity. His statement on the authority of Scripture would satisfy the most stringent orthodox theologian. He defends the virgin birth, the bodily resurrection, and the cosmic, visible return of Christ.

Why was the world of modern theologians so greatly honoring a man who was writing the kind of theology well over 90 percent of them most heartily disagreed with? That was my problem and dilemma.

———◦◦◦———

Barth intended to write an orthodox theology. He does not define orthodoxy as being that theology written by the great Reformed and Lutheran theologians of the seventeenth century. He has great admiration for some of these men, at times using the endearing expression "our orthodox fathers." Nor does he understand orthodoxy to be the writing of that one great definitive book of Christian theology to which later theologians could only add refinement and a touch of more recent learning.

In a conference with Barth in my year at Basel (July 11, 1958), I asked him if he were orthodox in the sense that he wanted to keep loyal to the whole Christian tradition in theology. He said that if orthodoxy were so defined, he would not object to the classification. Later I found out he said as much in the *Church Dogmatics*.[1]

Furthermore, dozens of paragraphs and sentences could be lifted out of Barth's *Faith of the Church* (lectures on Calvin's *Catechism*) and recited before the most stringent evangelical group, and, if the source were not known, the evangelicals would endorse the statements as solid evangelical theology. Or, to put it another way, no theologian in the tradition of liberal Christianity could ever write the things one finds in *Faith of the Church*.

———◦◦◦———

There are some obvious reasons why Barth is considered so great. His coverage of historical theology is impressive. No doubt if he had turned to historical theology rather than dogmatic theology he would have surpassed the great Harnack.

He cites the church fathers in their original Latin and Greek. He knows the theologians of the Middle Ages, and he mastered the theology of the Reformation. He cites Luther and Calvin more than any other theologians in the history of theology. But I did not feel that any of this held the clue to his theology.

Barth had a genius mentality. He could read rapidly, digest what he read, and profoundly critique it. In *Letters: 1961-1968*, he repeatedly remarks about reading through some large book on theology in one sitting. In a couple of instances, he read two or more in one sitting. In his university days, his papers ran from five to ten times the customary length. As a genius, he saw far more relationships in an issue than did people of even high intelligence. One of the most unusual experiences of my academic life was to listen to Barth unpack, layer after layer, some question posed by a student. I must admit that—among all the professors I have had in undergraduate, professional, and graduate work—I have never encountered one with a mind like Barth's.

Brevard Childs narrates one of his experiences with Barth. In a seminar on Melanchthon that was restricted to reading the Latin texts, Barth was challenged on one point of Latin grammar by a professor of Latin. The next time the class met, the Latin professor came armed with several Latin citations to prove his point. Childs continues,

> Barth seemed a bit flabbergasted at first, then slowly he began to make quotations starting back with Cicero, right on through the whole Middle Ages, from the top of his head. At the back of the room there was a big map of Palestine with the Dead Sea sitting there, and we thought that Barth slowly pushed this Latin scholar right back into the Dead Sea.[2]

As helpful as all this was, I did not feel that I had an answer to my problem. The solution came to me one day while I was lecturing. I was explaining to a class the importance of understanding the Enlightenment in order to understand the history of theology in the nineteenth and twentieth centuries. I was explaining how theologies could be classified by the manner in which they reacted to the Enlightenment. At that moment the thought came to me: *Barth's theology is a restatement of Reformed theology written in the aftermath of the Enlightenment but not capitulating to it.* His program had the following elements:

1. He denied that the criticism of historic Christian orthodoxy by the Neologians was valid.
2. He accepted all the genuine positive gains of the Enlightenment as they have been upheld by modern learning.
3. He rewrote his historic Christian Reformed theology in the light of the Enlightenment.

This is essentially a dualistic approach to the Enlightenment: Barth is both a child and a critic of the Enlightenment. The combination makes his program very difficult to get into focus. Barth disagrees with Schleiermacher, for he felt the latter had capitulated to the Enlightenment with reference to the substance of the Christian faith. Barth agrees with Schleiermacher in that Christian theology can be written only in the aftermath of the Enlightenment.

Barth is a child of the Enlightenment wherever it represents true learning and genuine progress in knowledge. He is a severe critic of the Enlightenment in its pretensions to final truth, to its perfect harmony with reason, and its criticism of orthodox Christianity. He lets the proud waves of the Enlightenment roll, but he marks a clear, firm line where they must stop.

John Baillie has Barth out of focus when he suggests that Barth ignores the Enlightenment and retreats behind it.[3] It is true that Barth keeps up a conversation with the whole history of theology, because that is part of Barth's understanding of the task of theology. But Baillie's observation does not come to terms with the fact that Barth's *Protestant Theology in the Nineteenth Century* is a product of Barth's intense study of the Enlightenment. In fact, the book has become one of the standard references for that period. Nor does Baillie's observation come to terms with how much modern learning is in the *Church*

Dogmatics nor with how much respect Barth has received from the children of the Enlightenment. Many theological specialists in all faculties respect Barth even though they cannot agree with his theology. In the conference for a new humanism held in Geneva in 1949 (reported in *Rencountres Internationales de Genève*, 1949) Barth more than held his own among Marxists, philosophers, theologians, and existentialists. If Barth had mentally retreated behind the Enlightenment, this never would have been the case.

------⋘⋙------

I don't think that Barth consciously intended to write his theology with specific regard to the Enlightenment. I have nowhere read in his writings that this was his intention. However, the impact on Barth of writing *The Protestant Theology of the Nineteenth Century* lasted all his lifetime. If one compares the index of names in that volume with the index of names for the *Church Dogmatics*, one discovers that there are few names in *The Protestant Theology of the Nineteenth Century* that do not appear in the *Church Dogmatics*.

Two-thirds of *The Protestant Theology in the Nineteenth Century* is devoted to the eighteenth century or the century of the Enlightenment. Barth knows that the modern theologian really cannot ignore the Enlightenment and its aftermath of modern learning. He also knows that the capitulation of liberal Christianity to the Enlightenment critique of orthodox theology was a fatal piece of theological strategy. Therefore, the only way for theology to survive in the twentieth century is to grant all that which is valid in modern learning but without the self-defeating strategy of capitulating to it with regard to theology. In other words, Barth *inadvertently* wrote a theology that is a severe criticism of the Enlightenment yet that comes to terms with the positive gains of the Enlightenment.

To put it another way, modern people are both scientists and sinners. Because they are scientists, the theologian must listen to them with respect; because they are sinners, they must listen to the theologian with equal respect.

To repeat an earlier observation, Barth is so difficult to get into focus because he is both a child and a critic of the Enlightenment. That is why fundamentalists cannot understand him. To agree with all the essential gains of the Enlightenment appears to fundamentalist mentality as already having given up the faith. Barth criss-crosses all the lines of their theological grid, so rather than attempt to really understand him they write him off as an odd version of neomodernism. Evangelical scholars are either puzzled or impatient. They are puzzled because he seems to be mixing oil and water. Or they are impatient with him because he doesn't say things that seem precisely evangelical.

We can illustrate Barth's duality as follows: As a child of the Enlightenment, he recognizes the development and legitimacy of modern scientific history; yet he defends the substantial truth of the resurrection narratives. As a child of the Enlightenment, he knows that we live in a scientific culture and enjoy its technological fruit (which he so lavishly praised after a number of serious medical problems); yet he scolds the scientists when they convert their science into a world view. As a child of the Enlightenment, he does not challenge the rights of biblical criticism; but he is a sharp critic of, and a dissenter from, much modern biblical criticism. To picture Barth as only a child of the Enlightenment and therefore as nothing more than a clever neomodernist clearly distorts Barth's theology. It is equally a distortion of Barth's theology to write it off as a ponderous effort to rehabilitate old orthodox theology. Barth's dual reaction to the Enlightenment makes it difficult to get him into focus. This difficulty is as common among nonevangelical theologians as among evangelicals and fundamentalists. It takes much reading and soaking in Barth's theology in order to more clearly see his methodology emerge.

One of Barth's most attentive students and admirers in the English-speaking world is Thomas F. Torrance. In his book *Theological Science*, Torrance makes the following comment about Barth's theology, showing that Torrance sees the nature of Barth's theology similar to the thesis I am advocating: "The theology of Karl Barth is to be understood as rethinking and restating of Reformed theology after the immense philosophical and scientific developments of modern times which have supplied us with new conceptual and scientific tools."[4]

Torrance himself wrote his *Theological Science* on the premise that Barth's theology is in harmony with modern scientific theory and is the one great scientific theology of the twentieth century. Similar opinions can be found in Günter Howe's essay "Parallelen zwischen der Theologie Karl Barths und der heutigen Physik" ("Parallels Between the Theology of Karl Barth and Contemporary Physics").[5] Besides theologians, physicians and lawyers also were reading the *Church Dogmatics* (for example, the notable Swiss psychiatrist Paul Tournier, who uses Barth for basic theological foundations for his counseling, and Jacques Ellul, French sociologist, who uses Barth as a source of his theological critiques of modern culture).

Barth is not alone in attempting to come to terms with the Enlightenment and modern knowledge and yet not surrender the substance of the Christian faith. In my opinion, Helmut Thielicke is doing the exact same thing in his volumes on *The Evangelical Faith* and in his smaller work, *How Modern Should Theology Be?* He is unhappy with Schleiermacher and Bultmann because in their effort to be modern they have lost the historic faith of the church. He is equally unhappy with the orthodox and fundamentalists who ignore the current cultural context in which theology must be written. He urges a program in theology that is anchored both to the great acts of God as recorded in the New Testament and to the modern world of concepts, problems, and dilemmas.

A long list could be made of theologians with programs similar to Barth's, such as Thomas F. Torrance, Emil Brunner, Thomas Oden, Hendricus Berkhof, Paul Holmer, Werner Elert, Heinrich Vogel, Gerrit C. Berkouwer, Donald Bloesch, Helmut Gollwitzer, and Otto Weber. Certainly one of the reasons that people such as C. S. Lewis, Dorothy L. Sayers, T. S. Eliot,

Charles Williams, and Owen Barfield still have a sustained hearing is that they never force educated people to choose between evangelical faith and learning. And certainly not all these theologians relate their theology to the Enlightenment in the same way Barth does. But in my opinion Barth's method of coming to terms with modern learning and historical Reformed theology is the most consistent paradigm for evangelical theology.

Some very sharp criticisms of Barth have been made by other children of the Enlightenment, especially philosophers. But, as W. A. Whitehouse notes in *Creation, Science and Theology: Essays in Response to Karl Barth*, seldom do these critics show that they have had the patience to read Barth through and give him an academically respectable hearing. On the more positive side are the critical appreciative essays in *Karl Barth—Studies of His Theological Method* (edited by S. W. Sykes).

Albert Bühlmann reports on an interfaith conference in Ajaltoun, Lebanon (1970), attended by three Hindus, four Buddhists, three Muslims, six Roman Catholics, and twenty-two Protestants and Eastern Orthodox. He begins the discussion by pointing out Barth's view of religion as the manifestation of human sin against divine revelation. Later in the text he comments, "Equally, very little was mentioned about K. Barth and his theology. His conception was quietly dropped completely out of sight."[6] But at that point the conference became superficial. Unless some assessment is made of the potential impact of human depravity on religious thought, we cannot assess the rectitude of our thinking. As Roger Mehl pointed out in his book, *La Condition du Philosophe Chrétien*, part of the genius of the Reformers was to investigate this very question. If the compass is magnetized, how can the pilot guide the boat correctly? Furthermore, such a comment does not reveal a knowledge of what Barth has said about non-Christian religions and Jesus Christ. This lack is typical of the usual superficial criticism of Barth.

The Enlightenment raised the issue of the relationship between obscurantism and Christian theology. It is interesting that the simplest definition of *obscurantism* given in dictionary and encyclopedia articles on the subject is that obscurantism is that which opposes enlightenment. The term was used at the time of the Renaissance for those who opposed the new learning and for Roman Catholic scholars of the nineteenth century who did not want the medieval nature of the Roman Catholic church changed. Oxford professor Charles A. Whittuck states that obscurantism is a special temptation of the religious mind if for no other reason than it is found more in religion than anywhere else.[7]

Obscurantism is the denial of the validity of modern learning. It is the stock method used by people who feel that modern learning threatens their beliefs. Obscurantism (secular and religious) has three characteristics: (1) It is selective, because the obscurantists must live in the modern technological society, which they can neither deny nor ignore. They therefore must select out those elements they must accept in order to live in the twentieth century. (2) It is hypocritical, for in every instance people who follow obscurantist tactics use elements of modern technological society to promote their obscurantist beliefs; for example, the telephone, the modern television industry, and modern office equipment with its electronic and computer technology. (3) It is systematic, for at any and all points where modern learning may undermine an obscurantist position such learning must be denied.

Whether said implicitly or explicitly, the propagators of the Enlightenment charged that one could not defend orthodox theology without being obscurantist. Barth challenges this thesis and makes the bold assertion that he can resist the Enlightenment at a number of points without being obscurantist. If Barth had totally yielded to the Enlightenment, he would have been just another (even though brilliant) liberal theologian. If he had not listened to the Enlightenment with seriousness and respect, he would have been written off as a learned but crabby orthodox theologian. Barth did not attempt to rehabilitate his Reformed theology by resorting to obscurantism.

James Barr's book *Fundamentalism* has disturbed fundamentalists and evangelicals. Among the many charges Barr makes, the overriding one is certainly that fundamentalist and evangelical literature is obscurantist. In Barr's opinion, obscurantism has neither place nor future in the world of biblical scholarship.

If Barth were an obscurantist, he never would have made such an impact on modern theology. But Barth is never obscurantist. He never makes slurring remarks about the theory of evolution. He never totally indicts biblical criticism. He never condemns scientific progress out of hand. He never denies philosophers their place under the sun. But that does not mean that Barth does not raise a critical protest here and there. For example, he never owned an automobile, because he did not think that the speed of transportation increased the quality of life. One could get all of life's essentials cared for by walking, by tram, and by train. Barth also gives a detailed dissection of so-called scientific materialism. Wherever Barth is critical of modern learning or modern culture, he bases his criticism on a substantial observation, and therefore is not obscurantist.

This avoidance of obscurantism can be explained also in terms of Barth's dual reaction to the Enlightenment. In all areas where the Enlightenment and modern learning offer real gains, Barth makes no objection and hence avoids obscurantism. Where the Enlightenment encroaches on Christian revelation and Christian theology however, Barth opposes the Enlightenment.

Barth's resolution of the problem that the Enlightenment posed for Christian theology is so radical that theologians of other traditions have difficulty interacting with his solution. All those theologians who in principle agree with the manner in which Schleiermacher correlated Christian theology with modern learning reject Barth's correlation even though they may admire his theological genius. This difficulty was transparently clear in the Karl Barth Colloquium held in 1970 at the Union Theological Seminary. Most participants were unrepentant children of the Enlightenment, and one can read very clearly between the lines that they were plainly confused in how to assess an apparent theological genius. They could neither identify their own unlimited allegiance to the Enlightenment nor the dualistic approach of Barth.

Barth's divergence from the marriage of Enlightenment and Christian theology comes out clearest in his conflict with Bultmann. Bultmann believed that the world picture of (1) the New Testament and (2) modern times are in radical contradiction. This belief is exactly the verdict of the Enlightenment. Barth replied that modern gadgets, modern technology, and modern scientific theories have nothing to do with the great acts of redemption accomplished in Jesus Christ. The bodily resurrection of Christ, for example, is independent from any world view. Barth stoutly defended the bodily resurrection of Christ, and those who doubt it ought to read his own words on the subject.[8]

Although Barth does not capitulate to the Enlightenment, neither does he ignore it. Therefore he has never been on happy terms with the fundamentalists. It might be presumed that the fundamentalists would rejoice that the greatest theologian of the century defended some of their doctrines. Furthermore, one might think that they would have high regard for the most sustained criticism of religious liberalism in modern literature, given in Barth's *Church Dogmatics*. It also should have encouraged them to know that the fifteen principles of liberal theology[9] condemned by the fundamentalists would also be condemned by Barth. On the contrary, the fundamentalists accepted Van Til's thesis that Barth's theology, for all its historical theological vocabulary, is nothing more than neomodernism. In fact, Barth's theology is more dangerous than modernism, for its use of orthodox terminology disguises the poison in the pot.

Barth in turn could not tolerate the obscurantism, antiintellectualism, and Pietism of the fundamentalists. Part of the blame may be on Barth's side, for he uniformly mixed with the professional theologians and the theologians of the ecumenical movement. I am sure Barth was as unhappy with the fundamentalists as he was with the theologians of liberal Christianity for their lack of real interaction with historical theology. In his programmatic remarks in *Evangelical Theology: An Introduction*, Barth insists that evangelical theology respect the history of the community as expressed in its creeds and theology.[10] If the church began at Pentecost, then it did not really begin with the advent of liberal Christianity nor fundamentalism. Fundamentalism is a regrettably unhistorical movement with reference to its understanding of theological history.

Markus Barth, Karl Barth's son, does make the interesting observation that his father was not the complete anti-Pietist sometimes presumed. The evidence he gives is the lengthy discussions between Barth and Billy Graham, based on the many things they held in common.[11]

In this book *Karl Barth and Evangelicalism*, Gregory Bolich shows how ambiguous a reception Barth has had among evangelicals. He outlines more than a dozen varying responses among evangelicals to Barth's theology, ranging from extreme suspicion and hostility to sincere admiration. One reason for evangelical hostility toward Barth's theology has been that Brunner's important theological monographs were translated into English long before Barth's *Church Dogmatics* (the systematic translation of which did not begin until 1956). Brunner makes more concessions to the Enlightenment than does Barth. He accepts much more radical biblical criticism and makes abrasive criticisms of fundamentalism. In linking the names of Barth and Brunner, evangelicals presumed that there was no significant differences in their theologies.

Furthermore, Cornelius van Til's book on Barth and Brunner, *The New Modernism*, was published in 1946. It proposed the thesis that neoorthodoxy was really neomodernism. For many evangelicals, this book became the official evangelical interpretation of neoorthodoxy, and for many it remains so even now. Hence Barth had a bad press among evangelicals long before his *Church Dogmatics* was translated volume by volume into English. In the writings of such popular evangelicals as Carl Henry and Francis Schaeffer, the bad press given Barth continues.

The evangelical response to Barth has not been either academically or ethically flattering. Why is this the case? In many instances, references to Barth's theology are repititions of opinions about Barth that are totally wrong. In other instances, opinions are expressed about Barth that can only be the result of the most superficial reading of Barth. And other comments on Barth's theology are the result of spot-reading in which the writer simply read Barth to find here and there an obviously unorthodox opinion.

Some interpretations of Barth are cases pure and simple of theological animosity (*rabies theologorum*), which produce the infamous "theological hatred" (*odium theologicum*). What are we to think of accusations that Barth's whole theological output is a hoax, or that Barth is the greatest (worst?) heretic in the history of the Christian church? Nor is it unusual to find Barth refuted by villification. Some typical misrepresentations of his theology are as follows:

First, Barth is accused of reducing the Scriptures to a *mere* witness. In reality, Barth has a substantial theology of the nature of a witness that does not reduce Scripture to a *mere* witness.

Second, Barth is also accused of teaching that revelation occurs only in an existential encounter. This accusation overlooks Barth's massive doctrine of the objectivity of our knowledge of God.

Third, Barth is accused of teaching that the Bible is the Word of God only as it becomes the Word of God in the existential moment. Later on I indicate texts in which Barth specifically denies that by no means can we ever with our most intense experiences make the Bible become the Word of God.

Fourth, Barth is accused of being an existentialist theologian. Barth specifically states that he repudiated his first attempt at published theology (1927) because it was too existential. Throughout his *Church Dogmatics*, he is constantly at war with the existential philosophers Karl Jaspers, Martin Heidegger, and Jean-Paul Sartre. He specifically rejects modern existential theology.[12] He also differs radically with such existential theologians as Tillich and Bultmann.

Barth is accused of being an outright liberal or at best a crypto-liberal. Such an accusation does not harmonize with the following: (1) The most sustained attack on liberal theology in the twentieth century is to be found in the *Church Dogmatics*. (2) The current brood of theologians in the liberal tradition are as stoutly opposed to Barth as he is to them. (3) The theologians who take Barth most seriously of all theologians are the Roman Catholic theologians, for to them Barth is an alternative orthodox Protestant theologian who counters their Roman Catholic orthodox theology.

Sentences that start out "Neoorthodox theologians say, . . ." when applied to Barth are uniformly misleading and do not accurately represent Barth's theology.

The manner in which Barth's theology is most erroneously represented and interpreted in the most misleading way is to cite his name along with that of Reinhold Niebuhr, Paul Tillich, or Rudolph Bultmann as if their differences were so minimal that for theological significance they may be ignored. This criticism is just as true of theologians on the other side of the aisle as if Barth and the other theologians were hardly a stone's throw apart. This lumping-together creates a major distortion of the nature of Barth's theology.

Any seasoned student of Barth's theology knows the radical, magisterial, and critical differences between Barth and his contemporaries. Barth viewed Bultmann as the modern version of Schleiermacher and therefore as a representative of the liberal Christianity Barth thoroughly repudiated. Those who have read Barth's letters and Eberhard Busch's biography (*Karl*

Barth) know that although Barth and Tillich were close person-al friends, Barth passionately pleaded with Tillich to give up his theology of symbolism. And any person who has read Reinhold Niebuhr's *The Nature and Destiny of Man* knows that what Niebuhr interprets as mythological and existential, Barth interprets as literal and historical (for example, the deity of Christ, the bodily resurrection, and the second coming).

The nonevangelical evaluation of Barth has not been too credible, either. From the papers and comments of the Karl Barth Colloquium, one would never know that Barth believed in the trinity, the deity of Christ, the incarnation, an objective atonement, and the bodily resurrection of Christ. In the ques-tion periods at the end of Barth's public appearances in Ameri-ca, the questions were rarely such as to enable the orthodox side of Barth's theology to emerge. Apart from a touch of hu-mor here and there, one would never gather from the ques-tions and comments that Barth had thoroughly repudiated the theological program of liberal Christianity.

When theologians who are full children of the Enlighten-ment ignore the strong orthodox elements in Barth's theology, to that same degree they distort Barth's theology. Or, worse yet, Barth is turned into a speculative or philosophical theolo-gian, a role Barth utterly abhorred. Or else non-evangelical theologians neutralize Barth's more orthodox theological con-cepts by partronizing them by listing them among possible op-tions in current theological discussion. At best Barth is treated as an eccentric theological genius who has had flashes of theo-logical insight worthy of attention.

And the nonevangelicals are just as guilty as the evangeli-cals in listing Barth with Tillich, Niebuhr, and Bultmann as if Barth's theology again were only a stone's throw from theirs. The evangelicals fall off one end of the log in interpreting Barth, and the nonevangelicals fall off the other end.

The critical issue is whether evangelical theology needs a new paradigm in theology or not. If an evangelical feels that the Enlightenment and modern learning have ushered in a new cultural epoch, which in turn has precipitated into existence a new and radical set of issues for evangelical theology, then such a person will feel the need of a new paradigm. If an evangelical feels that the Enlightenment is but one more chapter in the history of unbelief, then he or she will not feel that a new paradigm is necessary.

In a word, Barth is not for everyone. Persistent critics of Barth, such as Van Til, Clark, Henry, and Schaeffer, apparently feel that the older paradigm of evangelical theology still holds. But if one feels that the Enlightenment *did* precipitate a crisis in evangelical theology, then one is ready to read of another option, be it Barth's or some other theologian's, such as Thielicke's.

Of course, I believe that such a crisis in evangelical theology *has* occurred. Accordingly, those evangelicals who stay with the older methods must gloss over the problems raised by the Enlightenment, which opens them up to the charge of obscurantism. But the difficult, sticky, mean, hard, tough problems raised by the Enlightenment and modern learning, in my opinion, cannot be glossed over.

Evangelicals cannot ignore the fact that modern scientific history arose out of the Enlightenment and was made more precise in the nineteenth century. Furthermore, it embarrassed the nature of biblical history. In *Historiography Secular and Religious*, Gordon Clark reviews the problems connected with historiography but glosses over the impact of scientific history on the history of the Old Testament, the Synoptic Gospels, and the Book of Acts.

Evangelicals cannot gloss all that the modern sciences say of the origin of the universe, the origin of life, and the origin of man. Francis Schaeffer stoutly defends his view of these matters in *Genesis in Space and Time*, but he glosses over the enormous amount of scientific information that bears on those topics.

Evangelicals cannot gloss the monumental amount of critical materials developed by modern biblical scholarship. In *God, Revelation and Authority*, Carl F. H. Henry sets out his views of revelation, inspiration, and authority against all other options, but his monumental effort (four volumes) stumbles because he glosses biblical criticism.

The above evangelicals (and others) have specialized in critiquing the modern mentality, or "secular humanism." However, such essays in culture criticism always mask the amount of post-Enlightenment learning and scholarship the critic himself has absorbed. The very fact that the vast majority of evangelical schools seek accreditation is obvious enough witness that they too have come to terms with much that has followed from the Enlightenment. This too should not be glossed.

Some evangelicals have come to better terms with the Enlightenment than have others. My concern is that evangelicals have not come to a systematic method of interacting with modern knowledge. They have not developed a theological method that enables them to be consistently evangelical in their theology and to be people of modern learning. That is why a new paradigm is necessary.

This need is evident in the fact that so much evangelical scholarship is piggy-backing on nonevangelical scholarship. It does not have an authentic scholarship of its own. But Barth's paradigm has resulted in an authentic methodology. This is why he has received such a worldwide hearing even among those who do not accept his paradigm.

What, then, did I learn from research in the Enlightenment, the history of evangelical theology, and the theology of Karl Barth? I learned that to capitulate to the Enlightenment as liberal theology did is to betray the Christian faith. I learned that to ignore the Enlightenment and gloss over the problems it raised is to engage in obscurantism. Furthermore, I learned that obscurantism is a losing strategy in the modern world. I learned that those evangelicals who do not feel the shock of the Enlightenment gloss over its problems. Barth is not for everyone, only for those who believe the Enlightenment precipitated a crisis in evangelical theology.

I learned that, among all the options for correlating modern learning with the Enlightenment, the best is the theology of Karl Barth. I view such men as Berkouwer and Thielicke as offering other possible options. I learned, as others before me have, that we study Barth not to become Barthians but to learn new ways to maintain the old faith.

My purpose is to show how Barth's theology is a paradigm for writing theology in the twentieth century. One may be a five-point Calvinist, a five-point Arminian, or a seven-point dispensationalist and still learn to write theology from the paradigm of Barth. I am sure that it is not always possible to draw a clear distinction between Barth's methodology and his conclusions. But at least it is worth the effort.

Notes

1. Karl Barth, *Church Dogmatics*, trans. A. T. Mackay et al. (Edinburgh: Clark, 1936–1969), III/4, p. xiii. (Hereinafter cited as *CD*.)
2. Cited in David L. Dickerman, ed., *Karl Barth and the Future of Theology* (New Haven: Yale Divinity School Association, 1969), p. 31.
3. John Baillie, "Some Reflections on the Changing Theological Scene," *Union Seminary Quarterly Review* 12 (November 1956), pp. 3–9.
4. Thomas F. Torrance, *Theological Science* (New York: Oxford University Press, 1969), p. 8.
5. G. Howe, "Parallelen zwischen der Theologie Karl Barths und der heutige Physik," in Ernst Wolf, Ch. von Kirschbaum, and Rudolph Frey, eds., *Antwort: Karl Barth zum Siebzigsten Gebürtstag am 10. Mai 1956* (Zollikon-Zurich: Evangelischer Verlag, 1956), pp. 409–422. (Hereinafter cited as *Antwort*.)
6. Albert Bühlmann, *The Search for God* (Maryknoll, N.Y.: Orbis Books, 1980), p. 62.
7. Charles A. Whittuck, "Obscurantism," *Hastings Encyclopedia of Religion and Ethics*, vol. 9, pp. 442–443.
8. Barth, *CD*, III/2, p. 442.
9. George W. Dollar, *A History of Fundamentalism in America* (Greenville, N.C.: Bob Jones University Press, 1973), pp. 12–14.
10. Karl Barth, *Evangelical Theology: An Introduction*, trans. Grover Foley (New York: Holt, Rinehart & Winston, 1963), pp. 46–47.
11. Markus Barth, "Response," *Union Seminary Quarterly Review* 72 (Fall 1972), p. 54.
12. Barth, *CD*, IV/4, p. 5.

3

Getting More Specific

BEFORE I LOOK at particular topics in which Barth's theology may be taken as a paradigm for evangelical theology, more clarification of such a program is necessary. For example, it may be questioned if there is such a connection between Barth and the Enlightenment as I have suggested.

It is not difficult to show that connection. Two-thirds of *Protestant Theology in the Nineteenth Century* is devoted to the period of the Enlightenment. Barth tells how he mastered the nature of any century. First he would make a chart of the century. Across the top he listed (1) dates of world history; (2) events in the history of culture, art, and literature; (3) church history; (4) birth and death dates of famous theologians; and (5) the year in which famous theological books were published. Then he drew 100 vertical lines—one for each year of the century! Then he filled in his chart.

No wonder Barth's survey of the Enlightenment and of the nineteenth century is considered so masterful. In it, he included cultural history, politics, science, technological developments, and philosophical developments as well as the theology of the time. His book is uniformly listed as one of the primary sourcebooks for the period. In fact, his book has been accused of dominating Protestant interpretation of the period.

————◦≫◦————

Theologians in the stream of liberal Christianity have contended that the developments of the Enlightenment made orthodoxy an impossible option for a modern, learned person. Liberal Christianity was accordingly justified, because it could live at peace with modern learning.

Although that is the story most widely accepted, Barth did not believe it, nor did T. S. Eliot. T. S. Eliot (famous as poet, dramatist, literary critic, student of culture, and orthodox Anglican) did not believe that modern learning gave a mandate for liberal Christianity. He saw liberalism as the loss of spiritual sensibilities on behalf of modern humanity. Spiritual collapse produced liberal Christianity, not modern science and learning. Barth did not put it exactly that way, but he is in general agreement with Eliot. Contrary to almost all historians of the Enlightenment (such as Emanuel Hirsch), Barth believes that its theological development was a loss. The Neologians attacked and discarded the orthodox system. They were governed by a passion to be rational, critical, and modern. Barth states that there was not a first-class mind among them and that their reasons for abandoning orthodoxy were superficial.

This position also explains why Barth does not take the protests of the modern age with the seriousness characteristic of Tillich and Bultmann. For Barth, the contemporary rejection of orthodoxy is no more substantial than that of the Neologians. As mentioned before, he does not attack the Enlightenment where it is right, but neither does he accept its criticism of historic Christian theology.

He further writes in *Evangelical Theology* that the last thing modern man wants is the Christian Scriptures translated into contemporary jargon (*Kauderwelsch*, or gibberish, nonsense, jargon). Modern people are really interested in what the Word of God is in the text of Scripture.[1]

————◦≫◦————

My purpose is not to vindicate Barth's theology but to suggest certain ways it may serve as a paradigm for the future of evangelical theology. His theology is not a theology of glory, and it would be wrong to represent it that way. To repeat an earlier statement, one may be a five-point Arminian, a five-point Calvinist, a seven-point dispensationalist, or a five-point fundamentalist and still learn much from Barth's method.

Barth has his critics, and they should be heard in all theological seriousness. Lutheran Gustaf Wingren warns us that Barth's theology destroys the proper relationship between creation and redemption, and between law and Gospel. The Scandinavian theologians (for example, Gustaf Aulén and Anders Nygren) warn us that, while Barth's theology is not existentialist in the narrow sense of being built on one existentialist's philosophy, it is existential in its largest sense.

Cornelius Van Til warns us very energetically that for all Barth's pretensions to orthodoxy his version of orthodox doctrines is radically off base. Roman Catholic scholars such as Hans Balthasar and Henri Bouillard warn us that Barth is wrong on his view of natural theology and his interpretation of Thomas Aquinas. Gordon Clark warns us of serious departures from historic Reformed faith in Barth's methodology. Sytse Zuidema warns us that Barth reduced theology to existential prescripts and so robs it of its contact with creation and history.

Herman Dooyeweerd warns us that Barth makes a fateful division of nature and grace.

The criticisms continue: Carl F. H. Henry warns us that Barth's views of inspiration and revelation are defective. Donald Bloesch warns us of the weak spots in Barth's theology of salvation. Gerrit Berkouwer warns us that Barth's overpowering doctrine of grace has the power to eliminate the reality of our Christian faith.

R. H. Roberts warns us that for all Barth's denials, he nevertheless has created a vast metaphysical system and in his attack on natural theology virtually annihilates the natural order.

S. W. Sykes warns us that Barth does not recognize the many Christologies in the New Testament and the importance of that nonrecognition for any Christology. And Helmut Thielicke—and a number of other theologians with him—believe that, for all of Barth's greatness in rethinking theological topics, there is something fundamentally eccentric about his theology.

The list could go on. Each objection is a reminder that Barth's theology is not a theology of glory. His work is such a vast production, with so much rewriting of traditional topics, that it could well take a century of scholarship and scholarly reflection to assess it. All these criticisms come from serious Christians, and should be heard in any evaluation of Barth's theology.

I do not want to give the impression that a person may pick up a volume of the *Church Dogmatics* and read it with pleasure. Barth is difficult reading, for many reasons. First, there is the enormous bulk of the *Church Dogmatics,* running to thirteen volumes, some of them over a thousand pages in the German text. Second, Barth's style of composition has been severely criticized. His books are in the form of lecture notes in transit, and are more or less pasted together. This style is complicated by the German method of inserting short to extensive footnotes in the body of the text, in small print. Third, Barth can make enormous demands on one's learning, such as in his survey of optimism in the century of the Enlightenment.[2] Fourth, Barth can be boring. The exposition at times gets lost in itself. He piles words on top of words, sentences on top of sentences, and pages on top of pages. And fifth, the subject indexes of the individual volumes, and of the entire *Church Dogmatics (Index Volume),* are inadequate. They are oddly arranged and very incomplete.

Finally, interpreting Barth is wretchedly difficult. The major reason is that he may write on any subject anywhere. No passage that looks like his definitive word on a subject really is. Comments on revelation, or Christology, history, saga, the trinity, or man may occur anywhere in *Church Dogmatics.* He also corrects something he wrote in an earlier volume in a later volume; or answers a critic of something said in an earlier volume. This confusing style condemns his interpreters to have a firm grasp of the entire thirteen volumes.

———◆∽◆———

In reading comments on Barth's theology, it is surprising to discover how certain and how facile writers are in identifying the specific origin of many of Barth's ideas. Such identifications of the sources of Barth's thought are very risky.

In a lecture on biblical criticism, C. S. Lewis uses his own writings to make this point. In reading reviews of his own books, he found repeated references to the sources from which he derived certain of his ideas. Yet he could not recall one instance in which the reviewer was right. Then he went on to make the following point: All these reviewers had an excellent chance to identify the sources but nevertheless failed. They had gone to the same or similar schools as Lewis. They took the same or similar courses. They had read much the same body of literature. Yet they could not correctly identify Lewis's sources.

Although Lewis was making his point with reference to the critics' identification of biblical sources, the observation applies to Barth. For example, he is supposed to have derived his idea of revelation from Hegelian Philipp Marheineke, his idea of the sovereign Word of God from Georg Hegel, his distrust of natural theology from Albrecht Ritschl, and his antimetaphysical stance from Immanuel Kant. But all these aspects of his theology could be readily accounted for on other grounds, such as Barth's exhaustive study of Holy Scripture. He could just have easily derived such fundamental convictions from his exhaustive study of Paul's Letter to the Romans as he did from Marheineke, Hegel, Ritschl, or Kant. Or, he could have gotten such ideas from such thinkers but only retained them because he later reenforced them from his study of Scripture.

His lifelong friend Eduard Thurneysen warns all interpreters of Barth that if they see in him some sort of philosopher or metaphysician or system builder and not a passionate interpreter of Holy Scripture, they will misinterpret him.[3]

Evangelicals are quick to identify Barth as a Kantian and so dismiss him as one who corrupts biblical faith with Kantian philosophy. This charge is surprising, for in the approximately forty times Barth cites Kant in the *Church Dogmatics*, be is uniformly criticizing Kant, not admiring him.

The most significant thing about Barth's theological pilgrimage is his thorough repudiation of his own liberal theology, which was Ritschlian and based on Kant's philosophy. He turned from that tradition to the way of Holy Scripture, the theology of Augustine and Anselm, and above all the theology of the Reformers. The famous Harnack-Barth correspondence of 1923 sets out for all to read how violently Barth broke with his Kantian-Ritschlian heritage. In *Church Dogmatics*, one can read Barth's own indictment of Ritschl's Kantian theology, which was "antimetaphysical, antispeculative, antimystical, and antipietistic."[4] To turn around and charge that Barth did nothing more than resurrect Ritschl's Kantian program in theology and give it a few orthodox embellishments is nothing short of preposterous.

Furthermore, Barth specifically intends to write a theology of the Word of God, not one based on any philosophical schema. If he repudiated his first text on theology in 1927 because it was too existential, he hardly would have turned around and reconstructed one on Kantian philosophy.

I shall discuss his attitude toward philosophy later, but will say here that Barth believed that any philosophy and every philosophy could help in the interpretation of Scripture. One may well find Kantian or Kierkegaardian or Hegelian elements in Barth's theology. But to latch on to a possible Kantian element here or there and to totally write off his theology accordingly is not fair.

Unfortunately, the charge that Barth is a Kantian is used to evade some far more important things about Barth. Such a charge cannot disguise the fact that Barth has cited more Scripture than any other theologian in the history of theology—approximately 15,000 times, according to the *Index Volume*. This number excludes an estimated 2,000 exegetical inserts in the exposition. What living evangelical theologian has given that much attention to Holy Scripture? Nor ought such a charge of Kantianism obscure the fact that Barth had a massive knowledge of historical theology that more than swamps any Kantian elements in him. Furthermore, he respects this history and on many occasions uses the expression "our orthodox fathers."

The discussion in the past two sections has been about the interpretation of Barth. My contention has been that all of Barth must be read, as laborious as the chore is. The most common mistake of Barth interpreters of all theological persuasions is only to have read Barth here and there.

For example, if one's knowledge of Barth rests solely on comments on Barth in encyclopedia articles or journal articles or references in books, one simply has no idea what Barth himself is like. One literally must read two or three thousand pages of Barth to really get to know the nature of his theology. I stress this point, having read hundreds of secondhand reports of Barth. Clearly, nobody would ever know the real character of Barth's theology whose reading was limited to secondhand reports.

In much criticism of Barth's theology, I find a common mistake. According to Barth, the role of the theologian is to give a pure theological interpretation of a topic. However, in giving that pure theological interpretation of a topic based on the revelation in Scripture, Barth does not intend to rule out all other knowledge people may have on the topic. The common mistake in interpretating Barth is to presume that the theological interpretation of the topic rules out all other considerations.

This mistake is illustrated in the lectures and responses of the Karl Barth Colloquium, where so many of the contributors presumed that Barth's pure theological interpretation implied a negation of all else (such as culture, philosophy, or biblical criticism). For example, when Barth discusses conversion he attributes conversion, theologically speaking, to the Word of God and to the Holy Spirit.[5] He does not thereby rule out psychological or sociological studies of religious conversion.

Another example is Barth's theological definition of humanism (to be discussed more fully later). Humanism is to be based on the great humanitarianism of God in the incarnation wherein Christ comes on a mission of mercy and salvation. The philosopher Jaspers objected on the grounds that Barth was eliminating the good in humanism from the Greeks to the present. Barth's stance was that once humanism is defined and grounded in theology, then all the other goods of humanism find their proper place.

It is also the case in his view of creation. Barth attempts to discern and describe the theological dimensions of creation. He explicitly says that this does not compete with nor rule out what we may learn from the sciences.

The same is true with Barth's doctrine of man. Barth wishes to define human beings theologically; that is, how they are to be understood as they stand before God. Hence he gives a theological, biblical, and Christological definition of man which he calls *real man*. But some presume Barth has discarded all that we may know of humanity psychologically, sociologically, or psychiatrically. Not at all. All that we may know of humanity scientifically—the *phenomenal man* is not discarded. Barth's only point is that humanity can never be theologically understood by the way of the sciences but only by the way of revelation. If each understanding of man (phenomenal and real) knows what it is about, then there is no conflict.

Barth is pure theologian. His sole passion is the theological definition of a topic. But, having given the theological definition, he leaves the territory wide open for all other sorts of investigations. It is important to read Busch's biography of Barth and the letters of Barth to get the whole man in perspective and see what a comprehensive sort of person he was. Barth's intense focus on theological definition did not blind him to the broad stream of human culture and human learning.

———⸾∞⸾———

Something must be said about Barth and Neo-Protestantism. The term Neo-Protestantism was coined by Troeltsch to denote that movement away from orthodox Christianity that began in the Enlightenment and that spread out into all those different theologies we call liberal Christianity. Hence it is a wider term than either *liberalism* or *modernism*, which refer to theological movements of the last century and which are included within Neo-Protestantism. Accordingly, Barth frequently uses the term *Neo-Protestant* where an American writer would use either the term *religious liberalism* or *modernism*. Schleiermacher is the theologian who is judged as having founded liberal Christianity.

Barth was educated among liberal Protestant professors, especially such luminaries as Harnack and Herrmann. Herrmann was not a great scholar but he was a charismatic lecturer. When Barth commenced his Christian ministry in 1910 in Geneva, he admitted that his theology was that of his professor Wilhelm Herrmann. Due to a series of external events and inward changes, Barth progressively renounced his liberal Christianity. Eventually he became its most severe twentieth-century critic. A great book has yet to be written pulling together into one coherent story Barth's case against liberal Christianity. I think it can at this time be summed up in one assertion: *liberal Christianity is not Christianity as historically understood and is therefore not Christianity.* All the major concepts that formed Christianity as historically understood (such as the divine authority of Scripture, the trinity, the deity of Christ, the incarnation, original sin, and the vicarious atonement) were either outright denied or else so reinterpreted so as not to retain the original substance of the doctrine. In a series of personal and reflective remarks, John Baillie said that the cardinal error of religious liberal theologians was that they suffered from "the illusion of finality." They thought their theology was so secure it could never be challenged.[6] No wonder they were shocked when the massive volumes of Barth began to appear, in which the old doctrines they discarded were being so gallantly revived and their own theology was being brought under such unrelenting criticism.

One oddity of the history of theology is the accusation that Barth has founded a new version of theological modernism, or that he is a clever religious liberal hiding behind orthodox terminology. Barth several times mentioned in print that he had given up liberal theology. In commenting on liberal theology, he wrote the following (italics added):

> "Liberal theology" shall be given its historic meaning: a theology in the succession of Descartes, primarily and definitively interested in human, and particularly the Christian, religion within the framework of our modern outlook on the world, considering God, his word and his word from this point of view, and adopting the critical attitude towards the message of the Bible and ecclesiastical tradition—to this extent, an anthropocentric theology. In this sense, speaking quite frankly, *I can no longer be a liberal theologian*, though I was one, and an enthusiastic one, in my youth, as can be proved by literary evidence.[7]

It seems to me that we must take Barth's word for it or else accuse him of either a stupidity in theology (which can hardly be the case) or a theological duplicity (which hardly fits the man). Even such a stout critic of Barth as Gordon Clark gives Barth the benefit of a chapter on his criticism of liberal theology (*Karl Barth's Theological Method*, chap. 2).

It must be confessed that Barth has few close followers, regardless of his many admirers. Barth is out of harmony with all Old Testament scholars, all New Testament scholars, and all theologians who have capitulated to the Enlightenment as exemplified by Schleiermacher, Tillich, Bultmann, and American and British liberal theologians. The odd feature of the Karl Barth Colloquium was that so many of the contributors were such disciples of the Enlightenment on those very points where Barth was its severest critic.

Barth is also out of harmony with all orthodox, evangelical, and fundamentalist theologians who believe that coming to terms with certain aspects of the Enlightenment is fatal to orthodox theology. To repeat, Barth isn't for every evangelical theologian. But for those who believe that the Enlightenment created problems for evangelical theology that never existed before, his theology is attractive.

The manner in which theologians interact with the Enlightenment is so crucial to an understanding of Barth's theology that it must be reviewed once again, from a special perspective. The crisis precipitated by the Enlightenment is still with us and not at all resolved. The central problem the Enlightenment raised for Christianity is that of the authority in a scientific age of a book (the Bible) written in a prescientific age.

The crisis the Enlightenment produced can be illustrated by the publication in England in 1860 of *Essays and Reviews* (by Frederick Temple and others). It was a shocking event: it suddenly dropped on the English Christian public the kind of biblical and theological ferment that had been going on in Germany already for a century. It has been reviewed in great detail by Ieuan Ellis's book *Seven Against Christ* (named after the famous *Seven Against Thebes* of Greek antiquity). Using this piece of British theological history as a paradigm for the crisis created by the Enlightenment, note the following issues in this crisis:

1. Old and New Testament biblical criticism challenged the traditional and cherished views of Scripture, its divine origin, its inspiration, and its traditional mode of interpretation.

2. The rapid development of historical science led to many serious doubts about the historical integrity of Holy Scripture. Both Hume and Kant were widely read.

3. The universe as pictured by modern astronomy reduced Earth to the status of a particle in the cosmos and by implication trivialized both humanity and Christianity.

4. The new geology developed by Charles Lyell embar-

rassed the story of creation as narrated in Genesis 1, especially if the latter were understood as a scientific account of origins.

5. The theory of evolution stated in Charles Darwin's *Origin of Species* (1959) was a major across-the-board challenge to the traditional Christian theology of creation.

6. The scientific understanding of the nature of events, and the nature of scientific historical knowledge, created deep skepticism about the historic Christian supernaturalism and its doctrine of miracles.

7. The philosophies of Kant, Hegel, and British neo-Hegelians offered a better way of understanding religion. This path was supplemented by Schleiermacher's works as well as those of Samuel Taylor Coleridge. Sympathizers with German thought were called Germanists.

8. The standard great apologists of the past (for example, Thomas Jackson, Edward Stillingfleet, Joseph Butler, and William Paley) were both rejected and undermined by the emerging new opinions.

Today we are even more children of modern science, technology, philosophy, logical theories, psychological science, and mathematical logic. We are at the threshold of a great revolution created by the combination of the computer and electronics.

What is the nature of the authority, for modern humanity, of a book written in prescientific, precritical times? How can the children of the computer-electronic revolution admit divine authority to the Holy Scriptures written in much more primitive times?

———— ❧ ————

Schleiermacher's resolution of the problem of biblical authority for the modern age has been followed with variations from his day to the present. His resolution affirms that with reference to matters of fact or history or science the Scriptures are completely products of their times and without authority in these matters. In the sense that "all generations are equidistant from eternity," certain elements in Scripture are unchanged by the transitions of history, such as ethical concepts, the value of a human person, the nature of pure religion, the marvelous picture of Jesus, the vision of the kingdom of God, justice, existential insights, the quality of prayer, genuine worship, and communion with God. In these matters, Holy Scripture possesses authority, for modern humanity finds such concepts relevant to its own Christian experience.

Schleiermacher's solution can be expressed another way: in all matters of science, history, freedom, tolerance, critical philosophy, and literary criticism, modern mentality has prime rights over Scriptural content. Whatever authority Scripture may have, it cannot conflict with these prime rights, or we would be guilty of the *sacrificium intellectus*. However, once such matters are granted their rights, the theologian may begin the process of rewriting Christian theology for the post-Enlightenment Christian community. Martin Redeker is a competent scholar of Schleiermacher's theology but writes so sympathetically in *Schleiermacher: Life and Thought* that he masks the dimensions of Schleiermacher's reconstruction. But if one knows Schleiermacher's program, one can detect his procedure of reconstructing Christian theology.

This solution has two problems associated with it. First, it cannot really stop the attack of the Enlightenment and modern learning on the Christian faith. Nowhere is this more starkly and honestly faced in recent theological literature than in Gerhard Ebeling's essay "The Significance of the Critical Historical Method for Church and Theology in Protestantism" (in *Word and Faith*). It may be, he says, that if we start the burning process we cannot stop it until the fire has burned itself out. The critical-historical method is still burning! The credibility of the Old Testament is more and more shredded. Recent criticism of the Synoptic Gospels reduces the authentic materials to a few trivial things Jesus may have said or done and perhaps some authentic sayings of Jesus about the kingdom of God. The Gospel of John has been declared to be historically worthless (Ernst Käsemann).

The analytic, dissective, positivistic, historicizing mentality has won the day in liberal theology in the study of Holy Scripture. The mentality of affirmation, of faith, of commitment, of worship, of consent, of intuition, of imagination, of literary perception is allowed to feed on whatever crumbs the critical mentality may leave untouched. The character of modern biblical studies suggests that the crumbs are going to become fewer and fewer and that Christian theology will find its task reduced more and more to making moral criticisms of society or else spending its energies in a succession of theological fads. This trend is already apparent in such books as Deane William Ferm's *Contemporary American Theology* and Lonnie D. Kliever's *The Shattered Spectrum: A Survey of Contemporary Theology.*

Nowhere is Schleiermacher's contradiction so evident than in the schools of liberal Christianity where his solution is followed. A great tension exists between the biblical department, where so much of the biblical text is more and denied any normative status, and the department of homiletics, where the students are urged on to preach because there are such important things to say.

The second problem is that this solution costs its followers the Christian faith. Whatever theology the theologians of liberal Christianity propound, it is not the Christianity as understood from Justin Martyr of the second century to John Calvin and John Jewel of the sixteenth century. In many instances, the routine of systematic theology is replaced by lectures on the philosophy of religion or ethics, or else the course is no more than a survey course in current theological options. The theological agenda is more and more determined by currents outside the church than by resources within the church. However, competence in systematic theology and historical theology is currently demanded of doctoral candidates where some substance of historical continuity must be maintained.

All the various versions of liberal Christianity are taught by learned people. Their books reflect a high level of intelligence and extensive reading. Some are competent historians, and others are competent philosophers. I do not question motives nor doubt their seriousness or good will. I only observe and lament the tragic loss of historic Christian substance.

Roman Catholic schools and theologians have had their encounter with the Enlightenment. It first came in the form of modernism at the end of the nineteenth century. The popes of the time fought back vigorously and checked its advance for a period of time. The founding of the Biblical Commission was one means, and the necessity of signing the anti-modernist oath was another. But the impact of the Enlightenment in the form of modernism and biblical criticism could not be indefinitely stalled. From Leo XIII to Pius XII, biblical encyclicals were issued that gave more and more freedom to Roman Catholic scholars.

Vatican II showed that the Roman Catholic Church could not contain the Enlightenment any more than could the Protestants. The result is that today the diversity among Roman Catholic scholars matches that of the Protestants. This diversity ranges from Karl Rahner and Bernard Lonergan, who are attempting to give Roman Catholic theology a high intellectual defense, to Raymond Brown and Edward Schillebeeckx, who are attempting to mediate modern critical biblical scholarship with Roman Catholic dogma. At the far end is Hans Küng who apparently wants even a greater triumph of Enlightenment in Roman Catholic theology and church life.

The fundamentalists' solution is simply to ignore the Enlightenment and to continue their work as if it never occurred. This route commits them to the strategy of obscurantism. Evolution, modern geology, scientific anthropology, and biblical criticism are subjected to continuous castigation. The fundamentalist presses do not rest in turning out the literature of obscurantism.

Sometimes they do try to make hay out of modern knowledge. Harry Rimmer and a number of others attempted to show that the Scriptures contain anticipations of modern science. But that solution no longer works. There is also much reliance on the discoveries of modern archeological research but that foundation is laid only by ignoring findings that seem to counter the biblical record. Their unsophisticated views of revelation and divine inspiration inadvertently raise all biblical culture to the level of divine revelation.

There is yet another problem in the fundamentalist position. It involves a measure of hypocrisy. The fundamentalist must live in the modern technological world, which in turn is the gift of science. While denying the rights of modern science, fundamentalists abundantly use modern science in the propagation of their own views, as in the use of modern computer technology and modern television technology. In essence, fundamentalists do not have a theology that enables them to live consistently in the modern world, holding to fundamentalist postures and enjoying modern technology.

Charles Hodge is well known for the part he played in the Old Princeton School (1812–1929) and for his *Systematic Theology*. His solution of correlating (1) an inspired Scripture written in an ancient time with (2) modern knowledge has been accepted by a great number of American evangelicals. His thesis has two parts.

First, the authors of Holy Scripture were children of their times and knew nothing of modern astronomy, physics, geology, or biology. Inspiration does not reveal the manner in which the material world is put together.

Second, whenever the authors of Scripture do speak of factual or scientific matters or matters of the natural order, they are supernaturally protected from error, so even in these matters they make true statements.

Today the first part of Hodge's thesis would not be debated. But modern knowledge raises serious questions about the second assertion. It is not the simple task Hodge imagined it to be. Since his time there has been an enormous growth in the sciences of linguistics and cultural anthropology. There is a very intimate connection among a culture, its world views, the way it perceives things, and its language. There is some truth in the famous thesis of the linguist Benjamin Whorf, that all our thinking is shaped, determined, governed, and limited by the language we use.

Accordingly, it is very difficult to show how the writers of Scripture safely walk this narrow line, of being totally creatures of their own culture yet able to write their witness so as to escape their cultural conditioning.

World views, world pictures, views of causation, and the interconnection of things are deeply imbedded in the text of Scripture, which makes Hodge's theory very difficult to execute. Every single text that seems to affirm some element of an ancient world view or world picture (*Weltbild*) cannot be allowed to stand, for it would admit error in the text.

All evangelicals who follow Hodge's solution have a solution that the modern sciences of cultural anthropology and linguistics would say is impossible. Hodge's solution is more in the nature of an affirmation that he believes that there are no errors of any conceivable kind and from any conceivable source in Holy Scripture. It is not a working solution. In his popular book *The Battle for the Bible*, Harold Lindsell uses jesuitical logic to keep his Hodgian thesis intact. That book became the rallying point for fundamentalists and evangelicals who believe in the inerrancy of Scripture. The only manner in which the full theological infallibility and authority of Scripture can be maintained is to affirm that Scripture is free from every kind of error. Inerrancy so defined does not permit a person to make a distinction between the human, fallible media of revelation and the divine, infallible truth Scripture contains. And in the conference report *The Chicago Statement on Biblical Inerrancy* it is very difficult to see how the positive affirmations can stand in the light of the subsequent qualifications. Again, as with Hodge, it is more an affirmation of its version of Holy Scripture than a working solution.

Most evangelicals commenting on Scripture and culture presume that the issue of culture emerges only here and there in Scripture. Modern anthropological science, on the other hand, says that culture is on every page. Therefore Barth comes to terms with Scripture and culture in full harmony with modern anthropological science.

Barth's solution to the central problem created by the Enlightenment for the Christian faith is radical, unique, and creative. It is radical because Barth puts together affirmations other theologians on all sides have considered irreconcilable. Barth accepts the historical-critical approach to Scripture that Ebeling, to the contrary, thinks destroys orthodox theology. At the same time Barth affirms the full theological integrity of Scripture, which the fundamentalists think he can't do because he accepts biblical criticism.

The solution is unique, for no other theologian puts the items together in this systematic manner. Others approach Barth, but Barth is the most thorough in the execution of his basic thesis.

Barth is helpful because he offers new alternatives in coming to terms with old problems. He does not think that proposed Babylonian roots to the creation narrative militate against its theological witness. He does not have to absolutize the human side of Scripture in order to protect it as a vehicle of divine revelation. Barth does not commit us to the worn-out arguments of the past that nevertheless keep cropping up in so much evangelical literature. And he does not think that commonly recognized difficulties in a text prevent the text from being an authentic witness to the Word of God.

It would be helpful to compare the solutions of Hodge and Barth. Barth would concur with the first thesis; namely, that

revelation does not reflect on how the world order is put together. Barth would say that Hodge's second thesis contradicts
his first. If the writers of Holy Scripture are truly children of
their cultures, then they express themselves in the terms, concepts, and vocabulary of their culture. Barth does not seek to
save the writers of Holy Scripture form their cultures. They
wrote as anybody would write in their times and in their cultures.

Barth's positive thesis is that embedded in the culturally
conditioned Scripture is the witness to the Word of God or to
the divine revelation. The Word of God exists "in, with, and
under" the culturally conditioned text. (Much of this position
will be reviewed later, so I will not continue the exposition
here.)

Barth's solution has some distinct advantages. It does not
make the wholesale concessions to the Enlightenment that
characterized the solution of liberal Christianity. It does not
suffer from the internal contradiction of Hodge's solution nor
from the imponderables of working with that solution. It does
not need to resort to obscurantism in matters of science and
biblical criticism. At the same time, it stoutly defends the theological integrity of Holy Scripture as vigorously as any orthodox person would.

Barth knew all the objections to the historic Christian faith
raised by the Neologians and deists. He knew the objections to
orthodoxy, from Schleiermacher to Harnack to Bultmann. He
knew the "faith and history" problem from its inception in the
time of Enlightenment until his own day. He knew the critical
objections to Holy Scripture from Hermann Reimarus to Willi
Marxsen. He knew the philosophical attack on Christian orthodoxy from Hume to Jaspers. He knew the history of scientific
theory from Copernicus to Einstein.

In the light of all this, Barth returned to an evangelical theology. His final lectures given at the University of Basel were
called in their book form *Evangelical Theology: An Introduction.*
In this book he defined evangelical theology:

The theology to be considered here is the one which, nourished by the hidden sources of the documents of Israel's history [the Old Testament], first achieved unambiguous expression in the writings of the New Testament evangelists, apostles, and prophets; it is also, moreover, the theology newly discovered and accepted by the Reformation of the sixteenth century.

In the process of writing the *Church Dogmatics*, Barth maintains the decisions of the church expressed in the creeds of Nicea, Chalcedon, and Athanasius. He also maintained the full, supreme, material, and final authority of Holy Scripture.

One of the typical expressions, among many, of Barth's view of Holy Scripture is as follows:

> We must hold by the fact that the Word which calls us, the Word which forms the content of Scripture, is itself and as such the Word which exhausts and reveals our whole knowledge of God, and from which we must not turn one step, because in itself it is the fullness of all the information that we either need or desire concerning God and man, and the relationship between them, and the ordering of that relationship.[9]

Israel survived through all her defeats, apostasies, and captivities because of the constancy, the fidelity, and the covenantal love of the Lord. She did not survive because she had great philosophers or scholars or theologians. It is not different with the Christian church. There would still be a church if there had never been an Augustine or a Luther or a Jonathan Edwards. And there will be a church in the twenty-first century whether Barth lived or not. Modestly, then, I argue only for a good theology, a theology that blesses the church. I am not using Barth to uphold the ark of the Lord!

My thesis is that Barth's theology is the best paradigm we have for theology in our times. As a paradigm, it means that we do not need to defend Barth at every point. It may be that the best service of Barth to evangelical theology is not to give us a theology but to open windows to the fact that there are other alternatives to evangelical theology than the options that emerged in the nineteenth century.

I repeat what I have said before: one can be and remain a five-point Calvinist, a five-point Arminian, a five-point fundamentalist, and a seven-point dispensationalist and yet learn from Barth how to write Christian theology in the twentieth century.

Notes

1. Karl Barth, *Evangelical Theology*, trans. Grover Foley (New York: Holt, Rinehart & Winston, 1963), p. 35.
2. Barth, *CD*, III/1, pp. 388 ff.
3. Eduard Thurneysen, "Die Anfänge," in *Antwort*, pp. 832–414.
4. Barth, *CD*, IV/1, p. 380.
5. Barth, *CD*, IV/4.
6. John Baillie, "Some Reflections on the Changing Theological Scene," *Union Seminary Quarterly Review* 12 (November 1956), pp. 3–9.
7. Karl Barth, "Liberal Theology: Some Alternatives," trans. L. A. Garnard, *Hibbert Journal* 69 (April 1961), p. 213.
8. Barth, *Evangelical Theology*, p. 5.
9. Barth, *CD*, II/2, p. 152.

4

Preaching

I BEGIN WITH BARTH's theology of preaching for two reasons. First, it was a crisis in his preaching as a pastor that started Barth in a new direction in his theology. Second, it is one of the easier topics and forms a good introduction to Barth's theology.

Preaching was one of the greatest developments of the Reformation. The Reformers held it in highest regard in Wittenberg and Geneva. In Geneva, attendance to the preaching of the Word was a matter of careful supervision and discipline. Luther thought so highly of preaching that to him the Word of God was primarily the preached Word. The writing of the Gospel in the form of the New Testament was a concession to human weakness.

The Enlightenment produced a great change in preaching in contrast to the theology of preaching of the Reformers. Theodor Lorenzmeier comments on it as follows:

> In distinction to the preaching of the Pietists, the preaching of the Enlightenment attempted to respond to the spirit and culture of its time. It also attempted to bring culture and Christianity into harmony and to speak in the language understood by the common man. The preachers understood themselves as

teachers of the people, and endeavored to discuss concrete problems such as political questions.[1]

Schleiermacher's influence on preaching has been judged by some to be greater than his influence on theology. Schleiermacher was a distinguished preacher and preached regularly on Sunday for forty years. However, in both theory and practice his preaching was in the mode of the Enlightenment, not of the Reformers. In *The Christian Faith*, he treats briefly the theoretical foundations of preaching.[2] Preaching rests on the process of our pious and religious feelings coming to conceptual clarity and from conceptual clarity to preaching. Hence, Christianity has been identified with preaching. In practice, Schleiermacher's sermons were cultured sermons to cultured listeners. As great as they were reported to be in preaching craftmanship, they lacked the theological basis of the Reformers' theology of preaching.

The historians of preaching admit that there is no unified theology of preaching in Germany in the nineteenth century; nevertheless, there is no doubt that the model of Schleiermacher was widely followed. It would be difficult to trace any impact of Schleiermacher on American preaching, but much liberal American preaching was also in the mode of Schleiermacher.

The Enlightenment and liberal Christianity reduced preaching to a purely human performance. The sermon may be passionate or learned, clever, textual, prophetic, instructive, or inspirational, and may include some fine remarks about Jesus. Nevertheless, its theological presuppositions prevent it from rising above the level of human religious discourse. At best liberal theology attempted to claim that preaching was in the prophetic tradition.

The ultimate root of Barth's theology was a crisis in his preaching. Barth's lifelong friend in the Christian ministry was Eduard Thurneysen. Thurneysen says that there are two things about Barth that people must grasp or they will never properly understand Barth: (1) Barth's theology grew out of a crisis in preaching, and (2) the sole passion of his life was the interpretation of Scripture—no system, no metaphysics, no special theological stance—just the interpretation of Holy Scripture.[3]

In his biography of Barth, Eberhard Busch records Barth's agony in preaching as a pastor at Safenwil. He worked hard on his sermons, writing them out word for word but then delivering them extemporaneously. He left behind hundreds of pages of finely written script of these sermons, which are now being published.

Barth knew that there was something wrong with his preaching. Gradually the central issue emerged. Preaching in the tradition of liberal Christianity is giving a religious talk. It is talking of Jesus or morality or world conditions. The first sign of a new insight into the true nature of preaching was his famous sermon, delivered in 1916, "The Strange New World Within the Bible" (*The Word of God and the Word of Man*, chap. 2). This was followed by his commentary on Romans. He worked on that commentary with superhuman energy. Some days were twenty hours long. He turned over his task of preaching to others. Twice he suffered collapse from physical exhaustion. But when he was through he had recovered preaching as the proclamation of the Word of God!

Thurneysen describes Barth's method of sermon preparation. He laid out before himself on the table the commentaries of the Reformers, those of the biblicists of the following centuries, and then the modern critical commentaries. His passion was to find the Word of God in the text before him, for that Word is the necessary basis of the sermon. Thurneysen defines Barth's theology of preaching as follows:

> There is valid preaching only when it is understood to be preaching of the Word of God from the original document of revelation, that is the Holy Scripture which is inspired by the Holy Spirit who in turn makes it the ever new becoming of the Word of God.[4]

Preaching had to be a valid form of the Word of God, or else it was religious discourse. Liberal Christianity had a theology that prevented preaching from being the proclamation of the Word of God. In passing, Barth describes liberal preaching in America as "stupid and stale."[5] It was a preaching limited to "religious topics." In a letter written in the latter part of his life, Barth comments that he gave up "liberal preaching"— which he defines as "religious talk"—forty or fifty years ago.[6]

Barth set out an order of progression to show the theological basis of preaching. The first form of the Word of God is God in the act of self-revelation (for example, the incarnation). The second form of the Word of God is that of the written Holy Scripture. The third form is the proclamation of the Word of God. Each form is an authentic Word of God, and therefore a proper sermon is theologically and authentically a form of the Word of God.

Barth has a firm theology of the human dimension of preaching. To the observer, preaching is a very human event. It is one human being using a human language to speak to another human being. In this connection, Barth calls it a "free speaking." In other words, there is no divine aura about preaching that marks it out from other speaking. This means that the preacher is not heard because he is an authority figure whose words coalesce with the divine Word. Nor is preaching an alternative to the priest and the mass. There is no *ex opere operato* ("it works automatically because of its sacramental power") in preaching. Barth does not try to save preaching by making it some kind of numinous or unusual speaking different from all other forms of speaking—as so many lectures on preaching attempt to do.

Barth's theology of preaching also holds that there is a divine element in preaching. Walther Fürst attended one of Barth's seminars on preaching and took down two definitions of preaching that Barth dictated to the students. These complex, academic German sentences resist a fluid translation:

1. Preaching is God's Word, spoken by himself under the claim of the service of the explanation of a biblical text done in free speaking and directed to contemporary man by a person who has been called thereunto in the authority of the obedient church.
2. Preaching is the attempt in the church so commanded so to serve the Word of God itself through a person called to such service, that a biblical text is explained to contemporary man as it is done in free speaking an announcement of that which as if he heard it from God himself.[7]

From these two definitions, Barth's theology of preaching emerges. The sermon is based on the Word of God in the specific form of a biblical text. This text segment of the Word of God is to be cast in the form of a sermon relevant to contemporary audiences. Heard in faith, it strikes the listener as an announcement from God himself.

It is the Word of God—both actual and potential—in the sermon that differentiates preaching from all other forms of human speaking. By virtue of the Word of God in the sermon, the Holy Spirit may move! Grace may operate! The human words are heard as the Divine Word.

The sermon is at the same time a purely human product and a form of the Word of God. The next point is to examine how the human words of the preacher become the Word of God to the listener. This *event of transition* is a very unique concept in Barth's theology of preaching. True, stories and illustrations may help along the way, but the central issue is how human words can be heard as the divine Word.

1. The transition is prepared for by prayer. The transition cannot be assumed. It does not happen solely because there is preaching. Therefore, pastor and people prepare for it by prayer. In prayer, the petition is made for God to

activate his Word in the preaching. The preacher prays that his or her human words may serve the Word of God.

2. The transition involves the Holy Spirit. In the light of the teaching of Holy Scripture and in harmony with the theology of the Reformers, Barth teaches that the Word of God can be heard as the Word of God only by virtue of the ministry of the Holy Spirit. The Holy Spirit forms that hidden link between the Word of God and the heart of the listener.

3. The transition is risk, mystery, promise, wonder, and the impossible possibility. It is risk because the transition is never guaranteed. There is no guarantee that it will or must happen. It is mystery because factors are at work beyond the sight and control of humanity, such as the grace of God, the prayers of others, and the work of the Holy Spirit. It is promise because God has promised that his Word will always be heard in the church. Although preaching is risk, it is a risk within the larger circle of the divine promise. It is wonder because it is something to be wondered at that the words of one human being have been heard as the Word of God by another. It is the impossibility of human words of one human being being heard (fulfilled possibility!) by another human being as the Word of God. The impossible (that some human words could be heard as the Word of God) becomes possible (it actually happens!).

One of Barth's favorite analogies for revelation is that of the risen Christ going through locked doors. In ways that defy our understanding, Christ makes himself present. In the event of preaching, Christ comes to us under conditions that ordinary human reckoning could never identify as a hearing of the Word of God.

———⋙———

Barth's paradigm of the theology of preaching can be of profit to evangelicals because their problem is essentially Barth's problem. Evangelicals know that preaching must be more than ethical discourse, more than political advice, more than psychology with a touch of religion, more than clever talk on a religious theme. It must be a form of the Word of God.

Barth has tried to put together in a meaningful pattern the unrelieved, undeniable humanity of preaching, the necessity of preaching as an authentic form of the Word of God, and how the human words of the preacher transfer a divine Word to the believing listener. He has also tried to show the theological justification and status of preaching by tracing the unbroken line from the mind of God, to the text of Scripture, to the preached sermon, and into the mind of the listener.

Notes

1. Theodor Lorenzmeier, "Predigt," *Taschenlexikon: Religion and Theologie,* L-R, pp. 188–192.
2. Friedrich Schleiermacher, *The Christian Faith,* trans. H. R. Mackintosh and James Stewart (Edinburgh: Clark, 1928), pp. 76–78.
3. Eduard Thurneysen, "Die Anfange," in *Antwort,* p. 823.
4. Thurneysen, p. 834.
5. Barth, *CD,* I/1, p. 292.
6. Karl Barth, *Letters: 1961–1968,* trans. Goeffrey Bromiley (Grand Rapids, Mich.: Eerdmans, 1981), p. 33.
7. Barth, in *Antwort,* p. 141.

5

Apologetics

THE ENLIGHTENMENT was a period when the traditional Christian apologetics was subjected to devastating criticism. Many hands took part in this demolition, among the more famous names are those of Hume, Kant, and Voltaire. The attack was carried over into the nineteenth century, and by the time the smoke settled all the great books on Christian evidences and Christian apologetics had been discredited. The works of William Paley (1743–1805), which once were considered Christianity's most brilliant defense, were now considered obsolete in the light of newer knowledge. As far as the children of the Enlightenment are concerned, the older Christian apologetics and Christian evidences can never be rebuilt.

Barth knows this whole story. Although he refers to Hume only once in the *Church Dogmatics*, he certainly knows Hume because he knew about the connection between Hume and Kant. That which Hume started in a piecemeal fashion, Kant creates in the form of a majestic system. Barth knew Kant's philosophy better than any other philosophy. Kant attempted to show in a general way that traditional statements about the existence of God and the soul could not have any meaning. Then Kant exposed the logical inconsistencies of arguments for

the existence of God and an immortal soul. Barth knows both
this and all the other arguments against Christianity that came
out of the Enlightenment. He also knows in great detail about
the great Christian optimism of Leibniz and its satirical demolition by Voltaire.

As a by-product of his intensive research into historical theology, Barth had a good knowledge of the history of Christian
apologetics from the second-century Christian Apologists to
modern times. He thoroughly studied the great apologetic theology of Thomas Aquinas, and he was an expert on the
thought of St. Anselm. He was also a dedicated student of Calvin, and Calvin has a chapter (chap. 8) on Christian evidences
in the first volume of the *Institutes of the Christian Religion* that
sums up the standard routine of Christian evidences. Therefore
Barth's remarks on Christian apologetics are made from a basis
of firm competence in the subject.

Barth also knows the doctrine of human depravity, especially as taught by Augustine and the Reformers. Christian
apologetics cannot ignore the doctrine of depravity. Barth also
knows the great doctrine of the grace of God as expressed by
Luther and Calvin, and grace is another doctrine that must
figure in Christian apologetics.

The situation can be summed up this way: The philosophical basis of traditional Christian apologetics was undermined
by such people as Hume, Kant, Voltaire, and later Feuerbach.
Barth gave special attention to Feuerbach because he believed
that Feuerbach proved that without special revelation from
God all human theology amounted to nothing more than the
theologian projecting his or her internal thoughts into the external world. In this manner Feuerbach anticipated many of
the objections to Christian belief later posed by the logical positivists. The theological basis of traditional apologetics was undermined by the Reformers' doctrines of human depravity and
divine grace. Therefore our knowledge of God can only have
the character of a gift, not of a rational or philosophical
achievement. The center of this special, redeeming, gracious
knowledge of God is Jesus Christ, the hidden content of the

Old Testament and the revealed content of the New.

According to Barth, there is no sense in trying to revive any version of traditional apologetics with a little more philosophical and academic finesse. If there is a Christian appeal to reason, it must be set forth on other grounds than traditional ones. Traditional apologetics has lost its case to the children of the Enlightenment, and a reading of evangelical literature on Christian apologetics shows that this message has not been heard very clearly in evangelical circles.

Even though Barth discards traditional Christian apologetics, he cannot and does not avoid the issue of the truthfulness of the Christian faith. A discussion of his relationship to this issue requires a brief look into Barth's theological pilgrimage. In the 1910s he began to have serious doubts about his liberal theology learned during his university days. By the time he had written the second edition of his commentary on Romans (1922), he had given it up. When he was called to be a professor of theology, he began to search for a new foundation for his theology. His first published effort in 1927 he repudiated because it was too colored by existentialism. In his research and lecturing, he chanced on Anselm, the great theologian of the Middle Ages (1033–1109). He found the basis for his theological method in Anselm, and wrote a book on Anselm that he claimed was the happiest book he wrote (*Anselm: Fides Quarens Intellectum*, 1931).

Granted, he gave Anselm a novel interpretation. According to Barth, Anselm understands the Christian faith as a gift of grace. The experience of faith is at the same time an experience of salvation and illumination. Unless God moves toward us first in grace, we would never move toward God. Grace accomplishes what Christian apologetics cannot. By grace, by the Word of God, by the Gospel we are carried into faith.

Once carried into faith, the intellect comes alive! Now the Christian has the right point from which to think about the Christian faith. Faith does not stifle the intellect but leads it on, guides it, inspires it, encourages it, sets it in motion!

Those who charge Barth with being a fideist (one who believes that faith and faith alone is sufficient for all things, or one with a blind faith, or one who leaps in the dark) are plainly very wrong. Any patient reading of his book on Anselm dispels that notion, as do his repeated, clear denials of fideism. Barth's work sparked a revival of studies on Anselm. John McIntyre pays the following tribute: "Barth's account of St. Anselm's theology is the most comprehensive of all the writings on the subject and deserves the most careful treatment."[1]

In discussing the origin of faith, he clearly states that faith is not a magical quality given to people that is different from what people already possessed. He continues:

> We may also dismiss . . . the idea that faith is a blind subjection to a law imposed upon the will and understanding from without. [Faith] does not close our eyes but opens them. It does not destroy our intellect and compel us to sacrifice it, but it sets it free just as in a definite sense it captivates it for itself.[2]

Barth found similar thinking among the Reformers. Both Luther and Calvin believed in the power of the Word of God and the Holy Spirit to establish themselves in the heart of the believer. Both were theologians of the grace of God and of the Holy Spirit. Luther presented a great doctrine of the illuminating power of the Holy Spirit in *The Bondage of the Will*. Calvin's great treatment on the internal witness of the Holy Spirit became common Protestant doctrine. In their emphasis on the right role of the ministerial use of reason, both Reformers escaped the charge of being fideist. In a number of places, Barth plainly says that his Anselmic program of faith leading, guiding, and inspiring the intelligence (*fides quaerens intellectum*) prevented him from ever being guilty of the sacrifice of the intellect (*sacrificium intellectum*).

In summary, the grace of God, the Word of God, the Gospel of Christ, and the Holy Spirit—all interlocked—alone establish faith in the heart and mind of the believer. Once faith is established, however, the intellect is called into action and is summoned to exert its greatest efforts to clarify the different topics in Christian theology. (It may be said parenthetically that Barth agrees that there is such a thing as apologetics if one means by that setting out in proper order the whole program of Christian theology.)[3]

---∾---

One of Barth's basic presuppositions with reference to the truth of the Christian faith is that if something external to the Word of God is necessary to establish the Word of God as true, then it is greater than the Word of God. He states this in many ways and in many contexts. Or, one could say that it is a very weak Word of God that needs external supports. Barth's maxim is that what establishes is greater than what is established. But there can be nothing greater than the Word of God. Therefore the Word of God establishes itself. If the lion needs gophers and rabbits to announce his kingship, then the lion is no longer king of the beasts.

Barth takes as axiomatic that it would be very strange if Christians could believe the faith only if there were external assurances for it. If Christianity is tested for truth, then the test is greater than Christianity.

This conviction of Barth's can be set out in another manner, a conviction either that he derived from his friend Heinrich Vogel (*Gott in Christo*) or that is exactly paralleled in Vogel's book. Christianity is not a scientific theory to be verified by whatever passes among scientists as the mode of verification. Nor is it a metaphysical system to be established by some use of the principle of coherence or clarity of explanation. Christianity is about a Gospel. It speaks in the universe of discourse of God's justice, God's wrath, God's love, God's grace, human sin, human depravity, Christ's incarnation, Christ's death and resurrection, justification by faith, and so on. These concepts are the calculus of the Christian Gospel. According to both Barth and Vogel, that calculus comes through as true to the believer on its own terms, or it won't come through at all. It is a very odd maneuver to think that one first establishes Christianity as true in terms of some philosophical or rational or empirical test and then transfers that conviction to the truths of the Gospel. Oranges cannot verify apples. The philosophical calculus cannot verify the Gospel calculus!

This argument is not new with Vogel or Barth; it is as old as Luther and Calvin. Calvin in particular argued that the true knowledge and existence of God is gained through the Gospel. The Gospel is God's calling-card, whereby he introduces himself to sinners!

This argument also ties in with Barth's theology of the act of Christian knowing.[4] "Knowing is not the acquisition of neutral knowledge about statements, principles, or systems. Nor is it the passive contemplation of God. Rather, it is a process that involves the total person: his or her observing, thinking, use of senses, intelligence, imagination, will, action, and heart."

If there is a sustained section in Barth's theology on Christian apologetics, it is his treatment of our knowledge of God, found in *Church Dogmatics*.[5] To begin with, all the accusations that Barth is an irrationalist, a fideist, or an existential subjectivist, or that he advocates a leap in the dark are wrong. Barth develops a massive doctrine of the objectivity of the knowledge of God, for over more than two hundred and fifty pages (to which Hans Küng does not do justice in his evaluation of Barth, in his book *Does God Exist?*) This doctrine is not all new with Barth, for many of the seminal ideas may be found in Calvin and parallel ideas in Abraham Kuyper, judged to be the greatest Reformed theologian since Calvin.

In this section Barth spends a great amount of time attacking both Roman Catholic theology and liberal Protestant theology on the same grounds: both teach a natural theology, although for different reasons. I cannot reproduce Barth's argument here but can only sum up some leading notions whereby Barth establishes the full objective and true knowledge of God on Christian premises.

Some important elements in Barth's doctrine of the knowledge of God are as follows:

1. We know God only in virtue of grace and divine revelation. It is a knowledge in grace, for God is known only as he wills to be known. By implication, a knowledge of God based on divine grace rules out all knowledge of God that can be claimed by natural reason or philosophical theism.

Furthermore, in contrast to all other human knowledge it is God who moves toward the subject that he may be known. In more traditional language, this is called *special, soteric* (saving) *revelation.*

2. This revelation does have a content, a truth to it, which in turn addresses the human *ratio*, or reason. There is no existentialist nor irrationalist concept of revelation in Barth, as much as he is accused of the same.

3. Barth's doctrine offers a trinitarian and Christological knowledge of God. One of his major theses is that there is not a general knowledge of God that leads us to a more specific Christian knowledge. Rather, our knowledge of God from the start is trinitarian and Christological, otherwise, it is not a biblical knowledge of God.

4. Revelation comes into our world using human language, human imagery, human institutions, and earthly phenomena as its "language." It has not only a cosmic character (that is, it really comes into our world) but also an event character (and hence is not subjective). Revelation also leaves signs that it has occurred (Israel, the church, and Holy Scripture).

Barth's doctrine of the signs of revelation are very important. If he were totally Kierkegaardian, totally existential, or totally subjectivistic, then one would never know that revelation had been experienced by anybody else. But Barth does not shut himself up in that dark, windowless closet. Objective signs in this world point people to the fact of divine revelation: the history of the Jews, the existence of the Christian Church, and the Holy Scriptures. In fact, he quotes with favor the famous instance when the emperor of Prussia asked his court physician for the greatest proof of the existence of God. The physician replied that it was the existence of the Jews.

5. Revelation is indirect or veiled to preserve its spirituality. Profane people may not hold the divine revelation in their

hands nor in any way control it. This dimension to Barth's theology of revelation is not subjectivistic but is an emphasis on the spiritual requirements necessary for any apprehension of the Word of God.

Barth once likened a great theology to a great cathedral. It is a thing of beauty, and as we perceive the whole theology we have a satisfying experience of the beautiful. If Christian theology is like a cathedral, it then has a beauty or luminosity of its own. The Word of God shines in its luminosity. Christian dogmatics is beautiful in its transparency to the believing mind. If it fails here, it fails everywhere. One cannot save an ugly person with expensive cosmetics. Barth says in effect, *My dogmatics is my apologetics, my apologetics is my dogmatics.*[6]

This concept is another version of that historic concept of *autopistia*—a Greek word that means something is credible within itself. And so the older theologians had spoken of the *autopistia* of Holy Scripture. It carries its divine credentials within itself. Barth argues that the final apologetics of the Christian faith is the power of the Christian system of theology to glow, to radiate, to be luminous in its own light. To repeat, if it fails here it fails everywhere. Cosmetic apologetics cannot save an ugly theology.

Evangelicals and others have accused Barth of being an irrationalist. He is accused of flouting the law of contradiction (that a proposition and its negation cannot both be true at the same time). It is difficult to see how such a charge can be sustained if one reads extensively in the *Church Dogmatics*. Barth has always denied that he is an irrationalist. He has always argued that revelation is rational and that therefore theology must be rational. He has always denied the notion current in the Middle Ages that a proposition that was false in philosophy could be true in theology. His program is that of Anselm, in which the reason seeks clarification. If Barth were such an obvious (according to some, outrageous) irrationalist, he could not command the universal respect he has.

Barth honors logic to the limit. He says that he does not flout it or value it cheaply. In his old age he had grown weary of answering the question about logic, and to yet another questioner who wanted to know his view on logic he replied, "I use it."[7] Only in a few points in theology is one ever tempted to go contrary to reason or logic (for example, some aspects of the incarnation or doctrine of the trinity), but in those cases a theologian is being truly rational when his or her thinking is totally led along by the subject.

There is a measure of inconsistency in the evangelical charge that Barth is an irrationalist because he does not follow reason in total commitment. Missionary Raymond Lully in the Middle Ages had taught that all Christian doctrines may be rationally explained but that was due to his confrontation with Muslims who charged that Christianity was irrational. No other theologian in the history of theology has claimed that all doctrines can be fully rationally explained. Those of us who every year must attempt to explain such doctrines as the incarnation (two natures in one person), or the trinity (three persons in one substance), or the doctrine of original sin find ourselves always at the edge of mystery, where our logic stammers and stutters. And I do not know of any evangelical dead or living who could give a completely rational exposition of the incarnation, the trinity, or original sin.

It is common to accuse Barth of a leap of faith into the dark. Barth does speak many times of the leap of faith. One cannot read Kierkegaard and not somewhere use the expression, for it figured so largely in Kierkegaard's thought. However, Barth never speaks of a leap of faith *into the dark*. In fact, he specifically denies it.[8] He wrote in the *Faith of the Church* that "To *trust* in God is not taking a chance, leaping into darkness, or gambling and betting."

If he denies it, why accuse him of it? How could such a

dedicated disciple of Anselm ever advocate a leap into the dark? Faith seeks clarification, not obscuration.

It was Kierkegaard who made the expression "leap of faith" famous. Kierkegaard was an intellectual genius. He has been called Denmark's greatest theologian, greatest philosopher of religion, and one of her greatest writers. He is not a blundering irrationalist nor an irresponsible thinker. It was the function of reason to show reason its limits and where reason must surrender to the leap. In other words, only a brilliant intellectual rationalist could chart out the course where the intellect came to the end of its tether and must leap.

Kierkegaard had something very specific in mind when he used the concept of the leap. To leap is to accept a truth for oneself that at the same time stuns one's intellect. The one great truth of the Christian faith that stuns the intellect but that excites the leap is the incarnation; namely, *that this one solitary man, Jesus Christ, is at the same time the eternal God.*

In logic (such as in proving a theorem in geometry), a proof is worked out step by step until one reaches the Q. E. D. (that is, *quod erat demonstrandum,* what has been proposed has been demonstrated). But if a person skips one or more steps in the proof, that constitutes a leap. We cannot rationally fully explain the incarnation. Therefore, in the language of logic, one must make a leap to affirm the incarnation. In this sense, *all* Christians leap! Roman Catholics! Fundamentalists! Evangelicals! Eastern Orthodoxy!

If there is a revelation of grace, there must be a leap, for grace defies rational explication. If God works in ways that are unsearchable and inscrutable (Romans 11:33), there must be a leap if we believe in these ways.

Barth is perpetually worried that the Christian Gospel will be converted into a Christian philosophical system. He worries that faith (*pistis*) will be converted into knowledge (*gnosis*). This fear is one reason he is so apprehensive of Bultmann, Tillich, and Teilhard (he calls Teilhard's system a gnostic snake that swallows up the Gospel). These men convert a saving Gospel into a religious, philosophical system. Systems do not save; only the Gospel saves. When the appeal of Christianity is its appeal as a great intellectual system then faith has been converted into knowledge. But this temptation is strong, and it is strongest in Christian apologetics.

Barth worries that those who want such a rationalistic orthodox system will repeat the tragedy of the Enlightenment; namely, that the rationalism originally used to defend Christianity will be turned against it. To frame it another way, those who believe in a very rationalistic, very logical, very coherent Christian apologetics have not calculated with the possibility that their very sharp, critical, and analytical logic can be turned around 180 degrees and used against the Christian faith. It happened during the Enlightenment. The high premium placed on reason in defending orthodoxy was in turn used to undermine orthodoxy. Only in Anselm's program can reason be used safely, properly and "Christianly."

We can put it yet another way. A person who is not a Christian cannot test the Christian faith by logic, for his or her logic is imbedded in a non-Christian mentality. One cannot divorce the sinner from his or her logic, especially with reference to Christianity, where human sinnerhood is a cardinal consideration. Nor can one be a fideist and renounce all reason or logic, for that would make both God and his revelation irrational or something imperiously given. One must have a *Christianized* reason. Reason is Christianized by the grace of God, the Holy Spirit, and the saving Gospel of Jesus Christ. Then that Christianized reason can do its utmost to explore the depths of Christian theology. And this "Christianization of reason" is precisely Anselm's achievement and the point of the central failure of Aquinas's apologetics (and all apologists who follow in his train). And it follows that if our reason is *Christianized*, we can follow it without qualification, with no fear that it will ever turn on us (as it turned on some orthodox rationalists of the Enlightenment).

One cannot discuss apologetics without raising the issue of the function of philosophy in theology. Barth is accused of having the most negative, even barbaric attitude toward philosophy. The otherwise judicious John Baillie writes, "The Barthians, as we well know, will have nothing to do with philosophy."[10] This remark, and most of what one reads about Barth and philosophy, are wrong. Even competent philosophers who read a snatch or two of Barth on philosophy make most unreliable statements.

What are the facts of the case?

In *Protestant Theology in the Nineteenth Century*, Barth is completely at home among the philosophers, including such difficult ones as Hegel and Kant.

Barth's brother, Heinrich, was a philosopher teaching at the University of Basel. Barth contributed an essay in an honorary volume (*Festschrift*) dedicated to his brother on the relationship of theology and philosophy. In that essay, Barth sees the theologian and the philosopher as each having the same goal in mind (that of truth), yet going about their task in different ways. And he expressly says that theologians must respect philosophers and not think that they are superior to philosophers because they (the theologians) have the inside track of divine revelation.

In *Church Dogmatics*, Barth often dips into the history of philosophy, such as into a history of scientific materialism; or sketches out the systems of such complex thinkers as Jaspers, Sartre, and Heidegger; or makes a comprehensive survey of the complex history of optimism during the eighteenth century.

Whenever the issue of philosophy came up for discussion, he always said that students of theology must know philosophy, especially the history of philosophy. Competency in philosophy was part of competency in theology.

Barth greatly admired the sturdy biblicism of Gottfried Menken, who in our day would be called a fundamentalist and Pietist. Menken said his reading was the widest in the world: all the way from Genesis to Revelation. He claimed to read only the narrowest strip of literature: from Genesis to Revelation. Barth found one flaw in Menken's reading program: Menken read the Scriptures through Menken's mental eyes. And those mental eyes had philosophical tinting. The more we deny the philosophical tinting of our mental eyes, the more we fall victim to philosophy. Although we can never purge our minds of philosophical taint, we should be aware of it and confess it. The more we reflect on our philosophical coloring, the better chance we have of neutralizing it in our theology. To state it another way, only the one who has mastered philosophy has the grounds on which to repudiate it.

Barth discusses the role of philosophy in theology in his hermeneutics—which is an odd place for such a discussion.[11] He says that the second stage of interpretation is that of assimilation. The text is assimilated into the interpreter. But since every interpreter has his philosophy, that philosophy becomes part of the process of assimilation. Therefore the role of philosophy in theology comes under discussion.

The philosopher John E. Smith has examined Barth's view of philosophy.[12] He mentions this crucial passage in Barth's *Church Dogmatics* but utterly fails to properly assess it. Hence Barth's views on philosophy are constantly out of focus in the essay.

Barth makes three statements about the relationship of philosophy and theology:

1. No interpreter is free from philosophical presuppositions. Both amateurs and professional philosophers bring their philosophy to the text. There is no philosophically innocent interpretation of Scripture. Here Smith misses Barth's warning that the only way to cope with this intrusion is to be an expert in philosophy.

2. No human philosophy is the perfect correlate of the Word of God. Therefore no philosophy is the perfect correlate and handmaiden of divine revelation. Note that this statement is not an attack on philosophy or a demeaning of philosophy but, on the contrary, a profound *theological* observation.

3. Every philosophy may potentially illuminate the Word of God. This is the very point Smith underplays to the point of distortion. First, if all philosophies may potentially

help us to clarify the Word of God, we must know them all or at least a good number of them. Secondly, philosophies as a matter of fact have been of service in theology. Materialism warns us against any ascetic or gnostic or overly spiritualized interpretation of our faith, and idealism reminds us of the transcendental element in the human person.

———————◦∞◦———————

How are Barth's opinions on apologetics a paradigm for evangelicals?

1. Barth has felt the full force of the Enlightenment's demolition of traditional Christian apologetics. He knew his Hume, Kant, and Voltaire and anticipated the lingustic veto of the school of linguistic analysis.

2. He has tried to determine that method or manner in which Holy Scripture expects its message to be received as truth. In doing so, he has depended much on Luther and Calvin, whom he felt caught the pulse beat of Scripture on this matter.

3. In his Anselmic program, he gives both the proper ordering of faith and reason and the proper function or reason. He escapes the rationalism that would test the revelation of God, and he escapes the subjectivism that rests solely on religious experience. His notion of the Christianizing of reason is a most timely one for evangelical theology.

4. He insists on theologians being competent in philosophy without surrendering the priority of the Word of God.

5. He allows us to be free people in the kingdom of philosophy. How shackled are process theologians to Alfred North Whitehead! And how shackled so many theologians and New Testament scholars have been to existentialism! By being free from all philosophies, yet willing to hear and learn from all philosophies, Barth truly makes us free people in the kingdom of philosophy.

Notes

1. John McIntyre, *St. Anselm and His Critics* (Edinburgh: Oliver and Boyd), p. 28.
2. Barth, *CD*, III/3, p. 247.
3. See Barth, *CD*, IV/3, p. 109.
4. Barth, *CD*, IV/3, p. 183.
5. Barth, *CD*, II/1.
6. Barth, *CD*, IV/3, p. 882.
7. Barth, *Letters: 1961-1968*, trans. Goeffrey Bromiley (Grand Rapids, Mich.: Eerdmans, 1981), p. 294.
8. Barth, *CD*, IV/3, p. 544.
9. Barth, *The Faith of the Church*, trans. Gabriel Vahanian (New York: Meridian Books, 1958), p. 39.
10. John Baillie, "Some Reflections on the Changing Theological Scene," *Union Seminary Quarterly Review* 12 (November 1956), p. 9.
11. Barth, *CD*, I/1. pp. 723-724.
12. John E. Smith, "The Significance of Karl Barth's Thought for the Relationship Between Philosophy and Theology," *Union Seminary Quarterly Review* 28 (Fall 1972), pp. 15-30. See also "Response," the perceptive note by Robert Jenson that follows Smith's remarks (pp. 53-54).

6

History

THE ENLIGHTENMENT RAISED the critical issue of the nature of reliable history. In his chapter "The Conquest of the Historical World," Ernst Cassirer mentions the pioneers of scientific history: Pierre Bayle, Francois Voltaire, Giovanni Vico, Charles Montesquieu, Jean d'Alembert, Denis Diderot, David Hume, Johann Herder, and Edward Gibbon. In theological studies (*The Philosophy of the Enlightenment,* chap. 5), he notes as pioneers of scientific history Johann Mosheim, Johann Michaelis, Johann Ernesti, and Johann Semler. However, the scholars of the Enlightenment came short of defining scientific history. That development came in the nineteenth century and is associated with such names as Barthold Niebuhr, Theodor Momsen, Leopold von Ranke, and Numa-Demp Fustal, who was famous for his empirical dictum: *"Avez-vous un text?"* (Do you have a text?).

The concept of a scientific history challenges former methods of writing history. It challenges the notion that history is written to justify causes. Nor is it the function of history to write romantic summaries of some period in the past. Nor is history to be used to prove that Christianity or any other religion is true. In the scientific conception of history, the writing of history is to be governed by tough, critical empirical rules. All the sciences are to be drawn into historical craftmanship for whatever information they may supply (physics, chemistry, astronomy, geology, paleontology, anthropology, numismatics, writing materials, and so on). Special attention is given to documents not intended for history, such as diaries, letters, memos, ledgers, and import lists. It was also realized that the historian must read original state documents rather than accept secondhand reports. Hence, late in the nineteenth century the science of archives developed.

Typical of the new historian was Eduard Meyer (1855–1930). He knew Greek, Latin, Hebrew, Arabic, Sanskrit, and Egyptian. He was an expert in the history of economics and was a specialist in numismatics (coins). He has been called the father of such universal historians as Oswald Spengler and Arnold Toynbee.

Biblical scholars and theologians cannot ignore the present state of scientific history. The last great effort to write a theological history was that of Jacques-Bénigne Bossuet (*Discourse on Universal History,* 1681). Even such an expert on scientific history as Arnold Toynbee cannot satisfy the historians with his universal interpretation of history. This progress does not mean that all the problems of the writing of history have been solved, nor that there is one uniform theory of the writing of history among historians. In the writing of history, there is an element of imagination, of selectivity, of subjectivity that is not present in sciences. There must be a choice of a fundamental stance toward one's view of history for history to be written at all. The emergence of scientific history means that—no matter what the basic stance is, or the basic values of the historian, or the subjective element—the history written must come to terms with the basic tough, empirical, critical, sifted rules developed in modern scientific historiography.

I do not mean that historians prior to the advent of modern history had no sense of history. Obviously, such a historian as Tacitus did. Nor do I mean that all history written before modern scientific history is untrustworthy. On the contrary, most of our knowledge of the past is based on documents written before the advent of modern historiography. Nor do I mean that all biblical history is made ambiguous by modern scientific history. I do mean, however, that all history written previous to modern scientific historiography must undergo its scrutiny—including biblical history.

------------∽------------

Barth knows well the development of scientific history from the time of the Enlightenment to the present. He has studied the historical writings of such men as Baur, Hegel, Lessing, and Strauss. He has read how Kierkegaard attempted to solve the problem of faith and history. Barth studied under Harnack in Berlin, and Harnack was the prince of church historians. Barth made a special study of Ernst Troeltsch (1865–1923), who among other things was famous for his particular efforts to relate Christianity to scientific history. Barth taught at the University of Basel along with Oscar Cullmann, who was famous for his effort to correlate Christianity and history with his theology of salvation history (*Heilsgeschichte*). He knows of the critical-historical investigations of the Old and New Testament from the Enlightenment to the present. He writes to the widow of Martin Noth, the famous Old Testament scholar, that he has read everything Noth wrote.[1] He knows Rudolph Bultmann's reduction of the historical in Christianity to an existential concept of historicity (*Geschichtlichkeit*). He has also read Wolfhart Pannenberg's efforts in both theology and Christology in which Pannenberg seeks to rehabilitate Christianity on historical grounds. There is no issue about scientific history or critical history and Scripture or "faith and history" that Barth has not studied from the Enlightenment to the present. He knows very well Lessing's "ugly ditch of history," that faith is expected to leap!

Furthermore, Barth knows that there must be a real connection between history and Christian theology. The notion that Barth could live with a theological history (*Geschichte*) divorced from ordinary, empirical history (*Historie*) is a preposterous notion. Too much theology of Scripture is tied into history (as *Geschichte* or *Historie*—but more on this later). I am sure Barth is in agreement with the great Christian historian Herbert Butterfield that there is more substantial history in Scripture than scholars are accustomed to grant.[2]

The problem Barth faces is how he can come to terms with the development of scientific history and the historical materials of Sacred Scripture without (1) being an obscurantist with reference to historical science, nor (2) giving away the essentials of biblical history.

In the following I have attempted to list some of the leading ideas of Barth with reference to history, scientific history, and biblical history to illustrate that he is both the child of the Enlightenment and its critic:

First, *revelation generates history; history does not generate revelation.* Biblical history is the end result of God coming into human history. The process cannot be reversed; we cannot assert that we learn God's revelation by decoding it from history. The most recent effort to do so is that of Wolfhart Pannenberg, which Barth rejected because Pannenberg's project is impossible to execute.[3]

The reason that the reversal will not work is that any given historical event is capable of endless interpretations. There is no way in which the interpreter can know that his or her interpretation coincides with divine revelation. This dilemma is illustrated by recent efforts to reinterpret the history of ancient Israel from liberation perspectives to Marxist perspectives to Freudian-anthropological perspectives. One can only make sense of the biblical history by proceeding from revelation to the historical event.

Barth again and again notes that John 1:14 is the most crucial text in Holy Scripture. The incarnation sets the pattern for all understanding of Holy Scripture. One could never deduce the incarnation from history. If there has been an incarnation, one can know of it only by divine revelation.

Barth also insists that revelation has its historical dimension. He will not allow revelation to be reduced to mystical experience, existential moments, moral insights, or visions of social justice. The historical dimension is part of divine revelation and is therefore nonnegotiable.

Second, *the history that revelation generates takes place in our space, in our time, in our sequence of historical events.* Barth uses the expression "God with us" to indicate God's action in revelation is set in our time order, our space order, our event sequence order.

There have been some odd and erratic interpretations of Barth's view of history, both by evangelicals and others. Alan Richardson accuses Barth of creating a super history different from our plane of ordinary history.[4] Thomas W. Ogletree gives a much more accurate interpretation of Barth's view of history in his book *Christian Faith and History: A Critical Comparison of Ernst Troeltsch and Karl Barth.*

Some evangelicals have accused Barth of teaching that such events as the virgin birth and the bodily resurrection occurred in a special theological space and time divorced from our ordinary space and time. He is accused of teaching that such events of revelation occur in something like Kant's noumenal space and time, not in our empirical space and time. Such interpretations are eccentric.

Barth would be out of his mind to postulate two geographies, two spaces, two times, and two historical series, one of which was that of ordinary human history and the other of divine events. How could the virgin birth take place in noumenal space and time and at the same time in the body of Mary? Certainly Barth believes that Jesus Christ arose bodily in the Garden Tomb and in such a manner that one could touch his body, see his form, hear his voice and watch him eat food. All this is in our space and our time, not in some noumenal realm.

Out of the many references in the *Church Dogmatics* to the bodily resurrection of Christ, I select one passage for comment, as it relates to the matter of history. Barth writes that the resurrection involves definite seeing with the eyes, hearing with the ears, handling with the hands, real eating, real drinking, and real conversation. It is an event that "actually happened among men like other events, and was experienced and later attested by them."[5] The Holy Spirit descended at a specific place and at a specific time—in the city of Jerusalem on the day of Pentecost. Paul was visited by Jesus Christ on the road to Damascus in our space, our time, and our historical sequence.

One of the bases of this charge is that Barth is supposed to teach that there is a history (*Geschichte*) in which theological events happen and which is on a different level or plane or system of coordinates than that of our ordinary history (*Historie*). Barth may be wrong, but he is not mad. He nowhere postulates a kind of Kantian or Platonic world in which theological events happen and which hangs over our empirical world. By *Geschichte* and *Historie*, Barth means two different kinds of historical knowledge, not two different historical levels or spheres.

One passage in the *Church Dogmatics* is so clear that it puts the issue to rest. Barth writes that the event of revelation in Jesus Christ is not a Word, an event in a "spiritual sphere," but is a Word

> in the material and physical sphere, in the visible and palpable circumstances of the world around. Not merely in part, but totally, His Word makes cosmic [as over against "spiritual sphere"] history. And it makes cosmic history on this earth, in space and time, by the lake and in the cities of Galilee, in Jerusalem, and on the way to it, in the circumstances of specific individuals.[6]

The whole *Church Dogmatics* would be confounded and confused if it were built on the presupposition that *Geschichte* and *Historie* were two different spheres in which two different historical series were occurring.

Furthermore, Barth himself says that his vocabulary on history cannot be systematized, because he used different words or expressions at different times to make a relevant point. He has used primal history (*Urgeschichte*), revelational history (*Offenbarungsgeschichte*), covenantal history (*Bundesgeschichte*), and, to counteract Bultmann's view of existential history, salvation history (*Heilsgeschichte*). In the use of all these terms, he has never meant to take away from the in-this-world, here-and-now character of biblical history.

Gordon Clark devoted a chapter to Barth in his book *Historiography Secular and Religious* (Chap. 11). He works with more patience than does Richardson or Van Til, yet he comes to the same conclusion that Barth does not believe in the bodily resurrection as evangelicals do, but postulates this special space and time called *Geschichte* in which theological events occurred. Two things may be said in response. To begin with, Clark will not take at their face value the numerous references in the *Church Dogmatics* in which Barth explicitly affirms a bodily resurrection. No fundamentalist could use more explicit language than Barth in affirming a bodily resurrection. What could be more explicit than the following (italics added)?

> [The resurrection] did not take place in a heavenly or supra-heavenly realm, or as part of an intra-divine movement or a divine conversation, but before the gates of Jerusalem in the days of Tiberius Caesar and therefore in the place and time which are also ours, *in our sphere.*[7]

Secondly, to repeat an earlier observation, Barth may be wrong but he is not mad. It would be theological madness to postulate a Kantian noumenal world or a Platonic heavenly world hovering over this world, in which virgin births, incarnations, resurrections, and ascensions took place. That is why in the citation Barth excluded a heavenly realm, a suprahea-venly realm and the reduction of the resurrection to an idea in the mind of God—an introdivine conversation.

Third, *biblical history has its human side.* There is a human side to biblical history, and it is open to research by historians. The writers of the Scriptures wrote as historians of their times, not as the authors of the famous Cambridge Historical Series. The Holy Spirit did not lift the writers of the Scriptures out of the historical methods of their times. There is no necessity to overprotect the human side of the biblical history. Barth is not obscurantist on this point.

For example, the account of the exodus is open to investigation by historians, geographers, and archeologists, to see how much of the narrative they can reconstruct. And of course this has been done in great detail, as any modern commentary on Exodus reveals. But the statement that the exodus event was the result of God's activity in Moses and Israel is not open to the historian, in the sense that historians do not entertain the possibility of such supernatural events. The same is true of the resurrection. The report of the resurrection is open to historians, but the possibility of a resurrection is not viewed as historically authentic, because the assumptions of the historians do not allow for bodily resurrections.

Barth admits that mythological materials may be used in the creation account, even though the account is not mythological. He also admits that some kind of number mysticism enters into Matthew's genealogical table of Christ, but that does not detract from its theological intention. He also admits that the resurrection accounts are scrambled, but that does not diminish the witness to the bodily resurrection. Barth is patently honest and so comes to terms where the critical discussion is.

This approach is an excellent illustration of Barth's "split-ticket theology." He does not follow the old orthodox route and defend biblical history no matter what. He does not try to even out the unevenness of the historical record. He does not try to defend some version of the historical perfection of Scripture. On the other hand, he does not believe that historical difficulties in Scripture invalidate its theology. Barth has attempted to come to terms with equal rights for all: (1) historical science as understood in modern times, (2) the actual nature of biblical history as it stands in the text, and (3) the theological integrity of the historical element in Scripture. Both liberalism and orthodoxy fail to develop such a workable synthesis: liberal Christianity grants too much to scientific history, and orthodox Christianity defends the perfection of biblical history.

Fourth, *Jesus Christ is the content of biblical history.* It is one of Barth's axioms that the highest point of revelation should be the perspective from which all revelation before and after that event should be seen. By analogy, a sailboat is built up board by board. But the design was not made up as the boards were set in place. The complete drafted plans were in hand before one board was laid hold of. Hence the finished draft of the ship guides the placement of every board. The incarnation of God in Christ is like the finished draft of the ship. The Old Testament in anticipation of the incarnation was so written as to prepare the way for the incarnation. Hence it is not wrong to bring Christ into the Old Testament, because it is axiomatic according to Barth's thesis that the Old Testament was written Christologically.

Barth also uses the doctrine of the preexistence of Christ to substantiate his Christological interpretation of the Old Testament. The preexistent Christ is active in Old Testament history. Barth joins with the fathers of the early church and with the Reformers in affirming that the Old Testament is a Christian book.

If the Old Testament is not a Christian book, then it is a very odd book. It has many eschatological dimensions that anticipate some great action of God in the future—a kingdom of God, a new covenant, a Messiah, a resurrection from the dead. If the Old Testament is understood only as a body of ethical, national, and cultic teachings, then these eschatological promises stick up like so many unfinished stumps asking for completion but being denied. Accordingly, Barth radically parts company with both Jewish and Protestant scholars who see the Old Testament as self-contained.

Christ is, then, the hidden content of Old Testament history and the revealed content of New Testament history, and so unifies biblical history.

Fifth, *the relationship of biblical history to universal history is that the first is the meaning of the latter.* Barth's boldest assertion about history is that the tiny, slender thread of biblical history is the meaning of that wide river we call world or universal history. He comments on the enormous differential between the slender thread and the wide river.

World history is composed of an enormous glut of materials. Historians such as Spengler, Toynbee, and Hegel have sifted through it and tried to find the clue to its meaning. But to no avail. If there is any meaning to this wide river of history with its imponderable glut of materials, it is to be found in the biblical history that comes to its climax in Jesus Christ. If this is true, Barth claims—an amazing claim—then the meaning of every human being who has ever lived is to be found in Jesus Christ. Granted, only believers are conscious of this conviction; to the non-Christian, it is a secret meaning (but more of this when I discuss universalism).

Sixth, *the church and world history are likewise guided by God.*[8] Barth discusses the relationship of the church to world history to the providence of God under the Swiss motto that history is composed of the confusion of humanity and the providence of God. Because God is creator of heaven and earth, and the Father of our Lord Jesus Christ, history is unraveling according to God's fatherly providence. If, on the other hand, we try to make sense out of history from our human perspective we see only confusion. God's providential guidance of history is not an empirical datum; it is an affirmation based on biblical revelation.

How, then, is the Christian to live in a world that on the surface is marked by confusion but that underneath is guided by the providence of God? Each morning Christians are to pick themselves up and plod a few more steps on their pilgrim way. They know that they cannot decipher a neat little plan of the providence of God, for all they see in the daily paper is the confusion of humanity. Yet they believe that deeper than the daily news is the providence of God. For themselves they have found the meaning of their lives and therefore of history in Jesus Christ, because the secret meaning of history is to be found in God's purposes in Jesus Christ.

Barth is very stern in rejecting the historicism of modern critical studies of Holy Scripture. By historicism, he means the assertion that the real story is not the story as it reads in Holy Scripture but as it is reconstructed. According to historicism, the real story of the exodus is that which scholars create behind the text of Exodus. Exodus is a source for such a reconstruction. The same sort of historical treatment is given other parts of Scripture such as the Gospels and the Book of Acts. Barth's opinion is that when the books of Scripture are treated as sources they are denied their role as witnesses to divine revelation. The story behind the story is not a witness of divine revelation (more on this under the discussion of Barth and biblical criticism).

For all Roman Catholic and Protestant scholars who still maintain that Holy Scripture is in some objective sense the Word of God, Genesis 1–3 pose a very difficult problem with reference to scientific history.

These chapters mention the creation of the heavens and earth when there was obviously no human observer. They mention events at the beginning of human history when there was neither writing nor historians nor archives. No other documents or corrobative data enable the historian to double-check the historicity of these chapters. Yet these chapters are absolutely crucial to the biblical history that follows and to Christian theology. How does Barth handle these chapters?

Barth's treatment of these three chapters is based on two of his convictions. First, modern scientific historians will reject the historicity of these chapters on the grounds that they have no means of including such materials in their books of scientific history. Yet (second) these chapters are a kind of history, real history, which cannot be negotiated away as myth or legend or sheer fanciful, imaginative creation.

Scientific history has no way of speaking historically about a creation, about man's pristine relationship with God, or about a paradise of a garden out of which the original couple is evicted. Barth has no quarrel with this. These chapters are not history in the professional or scientific or empirical sense of history.

Historians work with historical data of all kinds—manuscripts, books, inscriptions, archeological reports, coins, archive materials, history of languages, and so on. They attempt to make a meaningful interpretation of these data. If there are no data, there is no history. There can be no data in the historical sense of Genesis 1–3, and where there are no data there can be no writing of history.

But there is history here. The world was created. Humanity did appear as God's creature. There was the event of sin and the resulting enmity between humanity and God. Barth invokes the concept of saga for this history, which he borrows from old Icelandic and Norse stories. Barth has a very special definition of saga, and he repeatedly expresses anger at those who do not take the trouble to understand precisely what he means. Saga is a special kind of historical reporting. Saga deals with real events in real space and in real time just as scientific history. But it deals with those kinds of events that elude scientific history.

Saga deals with prehistory (before the usual means of writing history could occur) or primal history (*Urgeschichte*—the history at the root of all history, hence beyond ordinary historiography). Therefore it is a history that is in need of a special classification, a special category. It is a historical category that cannot be compared to anything else. The Encyclopaedia Britannica defines saga as follows:

> In a stricter sense, however, the term saga is confined to legendary and historical fictions, in which the author has attempted an imaginative reconstruction of the past and organized the subject matter according to certain esthetic principles.[9]

Although Barth doesn't mention Roman Catholic scholars, it is apparent to me that he is capitalizing on some of their ideas. Roman Catholic theology is officially committed to the Adam materials of Holy Scripture, such as Genesis 3 and Romans 5:12-21. As a result, a large body of Roman Catholic materials have been produced on this subject—most in German, but some in English. The issues have been masterfully reviewed in Urs Baumann, *Erbsünde: Ihr traditionelles Verständnis in der Krise heutiger Theologie* ("Original Sin: Its Traditional Understanding in the Crisis of Contemporary Theology"). Another book that attempts to deal with the interpretation of Genesis 1-3 and the problems created by modern historical science is that of Henricus Rencken's (*Israel's Concepts of the Beginning: The Theology of Genesis 1-3*).

The problem is that the story of the origin of the universe, life, and humanity as recorded in Genesis 1-3 is so vastly different from the story told by modern astronomy, geology, biology, paleontology, and physical anthropology. The problem that faces the Roman Catholic scholars, Barth, and evangelicals is "How can both stories be true at the same time?"

The point of beginning in understanding Genesis 1-3 is that the passage was written by a scribe in Israel. If the passage has any historical substance, it is that of a very unique recovery of the past. Both the Roman Catholic scholars and Barth consider Genesis 1-3 as produced by divine revelation and divine inspiration. But the question is "How is such prehistory recovered?" It is recovered by—to use the term in the literature—*ideal reconstruction* (which could also be another definition of a saga).

1. The language of the text is Hebrew; the flora and fauna or "backdrop" of the passage is Palestinian; the vocabulary and conceptual range is Hebrew; the overall geographical setting is Mid-Eastern. In a word, it is an *ideal reconstruction* that takes place in Israel and therefore bears Israel's cultural stamp.

2. It is prophecy in reverse. Just as the prophets spoke of future judgment and/or salvation in terms of Hebrew culture, concepts, and history, so the past history is recovered by a gift of prophecy in reverse. It is the gift of the vision of the Lord to see into the past.

3. It is an exercise in divining. To divine something is to attempt by imagination to reconstruct events where the historian (in this case) was not present. Hence it was a Hebrew, with the rich Hebrew theological heritage from the patriarchs to the time of his writing of Genesis, that was in his mind as he attempted to reconstruct the past.

4. Its literary genre is more poetic (the adjective, more than the noun) than any other.

5. The purpose of it is basically theological; namely, to show that with the first person (*homo sapiens sapiens*) there is also the beginning of sin. Creation, the origin of humanity, and the emergence of sin are all bound together in one history.

Hans-Joachim Kraus surveyed Barth's effort to restate the case for biblical history. Although he did not have Barth's treatment of Genesis 1–3 particularly in view, I think his words would include it:

> The precision and clarity with which Barth thinks of the revelation fulfilled in Christ then related to history is in the history of Protestant dogmatics without example. In this way can the reality of the special history of God only be recognized.[10]

------◆------

Roman Catholic theologians, Karl Barth, and evangelicals all know that modern scientific history and other sciences have created this crisis in Christian theology. History and theology are woven so tightly together in Holy Scripture that the historical basis of revelation and redemption cannot be separated. Yet modern scientific history and the other sciences have challenged both the history and the facts of Genesis 1–3.

One response of evangelicals is to declare the passage to be solid, factual history. It is as much "out there"—that is, objective, reportable events—as anything else in secular history. Only, in the case of Genesis 1–3, God is acting as the reporter as he reveals the events to Moses who in turn writes them down. If there is a conflict between Genesis 1–3 and the sciences, it is then either a choice between the inerrant Word of God and the sinful opinions of humanity; or between the inerrant Word of God and the hypothetical guessing of scientists. But either way the Scripture is right, and the scientists are wrong.

The basic problem with such a stance is that it brings us back to the issue of obscurantism. Such defenders of the biblical record must deny an imposing amount of material accepted by the worldwide community of historians and scientists. The evangelical cannot afford to solve this problem by disguised or outright obscurantism.

If Barth does nothing else, he shows us that this difficulty can be handled without being an obscurantist fundamentalist nor a concessive liberal. He neither denies modern learning, nor does he surrender the theological revelation of the text.

1. First of all, with reference to the matter of evolution or creation he has expressed himself on the subject in a simple, direct manner to his grandniece, Christine Barth.[11] He says both the biblical creation account and the evolutionary account are true in their own way. The source of one is divine revelation, and the source of the other is human, scientific speculation. But one must never be forced to choose between them because they are two different kinds of accounts. If we are forced to choose between them, then we lose what the other one has to tell us.

2. In his concept of saga, Barth has done more creative thinking than anybody else on the historical nature of prehistorical materials. A saga is not a myth nor a legend nor an imaginative fabrication. It is a genre of real history but the kind of history that is not manageable by the ordinary methods of historiography. If one rejects Barth's concept of saga, then one must develop one's own version of a history being written when there were as yet no historians, records, or manuscripts.

3. Barth does not counter scientific history. As a child of the Enlightenment, he grants it its place among human studies. Nor does he try to spare the historical aspect of Scripture from historical, scientific scrutiny. He objects, however, to historicism where the historical explanation claims to replace the biblical witness.

4. He does try to relate theology and revelation to history in such a way that the genuine historical factuality of the event of revelation is maintained but maintained in such a way that it in turn does not become the possession of the historian.

Notes

1. Karl Barth, *Letters: 1961-1968*, trans. Goeffrey Bromiley (Grand Rapids, Mich.: Eerdmans, 1981), p. 301.
2. See William A. Speck, "The Legacy of a Christian Historian," *A Christian View of History?* George Maksolen and Frank Roberts, eds. (Grand Rapids, Mich.: Eerdmans, 1975), pp. 99-118.
3. See exchange of letters between Karl Barth and Wolfhart Pannenberg, in Barth, *Letters: 1961-1968*, pp. 177, 360.
4. Alan Richardson, *History Sacred and Profane* (London: SCM Press, 1964), pp. 127-139.
5. Barth, *CD*, IV/2, p. 143.
6. Barth, *CD*, IV/2, pp. 209-210.
7. Barth, *CD*, IV/3, p. 298.
8. Barth, *CD*, IV/3.
9. Encyclopaedia Britannica, 15th ed., vol. 16, p. 145.
10. Hans-Joachim Kraus, "Das Problem der Heilsgeschichte in der Kirchlichen Dogmatik," in *Antwort*, p. 76.
11. Barth, *Letters: 1961-1968*, p. 184.

7

The Word of God

DURING THE ENLIGHTENMENT, the orthodox view of the divine inspiration of Scripture was attacked, especially as it was developed in the seventeenth century. Increased knowledge of peoples outside of Europe and America, growth in scientific knowledge, developments in philosophy, and innovations in technology together created a mood that was not congenial toward a book that claimed to be the veritable inspired Word of God. Also during the Enlightenment, biblical criticism with a skeptical bent to it arose, especially among the Neologians (for example, Johann Semler and Johann Ernesti). The clash between those who held to the traditional doctrine of inspiration and the critics was inevitable. It eventually led to the heresy trials of William Robertson Smith (1846-1894) in Scotland and Charles Augustus Briggs (1841-1912) in America. And the conflict continues unabated until the present. How can the church to continue to affirm that Holy Scripture is the inspired Word of God in the face of such continued challenge from critical studies of Holy Scripture? More particularly, how can evangelicals retain their faith in the divine inspiration and indefectible authority of Holy Scripture when the currents of biblical criticism run so strongly and so persistently against such belief?

------∽◇∽------

Having studied the Enlightenment in such great detail, its theologians, its Neologians, and its biblical scholars Barth is well acquainted with this story. He knows all the objections to the inspiration of Holy Scripture raised by the Neologians. He also studied such radical biblical critics as David Strauss, Ferdinand Baur, and Hermann Reimarus. He also knows the contemporary status of both Old and New Testament criticism.

Barth's peculiar position is that he does not dismiss the critical study of Scripture, as do so many evangelicals and fundamentalists. Granted, the latter write books on biblical criticism and teach classes on Old and New Testament introduction, but they always do so very safely and properly. Barth does not believe that the divinity of Scripture can be protected by ruling all biblical criticism out of court. Nor does Barth capitulate to the Neologians of the eighteenth century or to the biblical critics of the twentieth century. He maintains the full theological integrity of Holy Scripture. Hence he puzzles both the evangelicals and the biblical critics.

How can Barth affirm a position that involves the mutual affirmation of the opposites, according to evangelicals to the right and biblical critics to the left?

Barth's thesis creates a *diastasis* (distance), an interval between the Word of God and the text of Holy Scripture. By creating this interval, Barth is able to grant historical and literary criticism of the text its rightful place but at the same time manages not to surrender the theological integrity of Holy Scripture.

------∽◇∽------

Let us compare the older orthodox strategy with Barth's. The older strategy (and its current defenders) proposed an inerrant original text. Whatever problems there were in the current text would not be found in the original text. Furthermore, even though theologians differed they all took as the point of dead reckoning the inerrant, infallible Scripture. Even though the text is corrupt and interpretations differ, there is profound

consolation in that the theologians are working from an infallible, inerrant source or infallibly drawn benchmark.

Barth pushes this infallible, inerrant point of reference back
one stage to God himself. God is infallible, inerrant, indefectible, rational, and free from contradiction or paradox in his inner being.[1] The primal meaning of the Word of God is God in
his self-disclosure; God in his act of revelation, which is (as it
originates in God) infallible, inerrant, and indefectible.

However, when the Word of God comes into the human
sphere it undergoes a diffraction.

The Word of God comes to the prophet or apostle in his
language. No human language is a perfect mirror in which the
Word of God is perfectly reflected. Hence a *diastasis* occurs at
the point of language. Barth notes that the Hegelians presumed there was a pure conceptual language that would be the
language of truth.[2] It is amazing how the current evangelical
stress on propositional revelation is but an alternate version of
this Hegelian theory of a pure conceptual language. In this
pure conceptual language of truth (or propositions!), there
would be no diastasis between the concept in the mind of the
speaker and his or her spoken or written words. Barth also
could have referred to efforts among the positivistic philosophers of the twentieth century, who thought that they could
create a pure language that would assert the truth and only the
truth.

Barth has the linguists on his side when he says no such
perfection in language can be achieved. He also chides biblical
orthodoxy for not coming to terms with the limitations of all
human language. In that Hebrew and Greek also share in the
limitation of all languages, Holy Scripture too must reflect a
diastasis between the original Word of God and its witness in
the Hebrew and Greek texts.

Although it is true that Barth believes that there is a diastasis between the Word of God as God gives it and its expression
in human language, he is not skeptical toward language. There
is a difference between the concept of a diastasis and the skeptical view that language may not be able to bear the Word of

God. Barth's perpetual repetition that revelation is witnessed in Scripture, or Scripture is the witness to revelation, means that language is adequate for the purposes of revelation. In his remarks at the University of Chicago, he specifically said that Holy Scripture has always adequately functioned in the church to bring people to a saving knowledge of Jesus Christ.

The Word of God comes to the prophet, who is also a person existing in a given culture; hence the Word of God is stated in the terms and concepts of the prophet's culture. This translation creates a diastasis between the original Word of God and its cultural expression in Holy Scripture.

The Word of God comes to the prophet and apostles, who, like all other people, are sinful. The sinful human mind does not reflect the pure Word of God, hence another diastasis emerges at this point.

Barth uses other expressions to indicate the interval between the original Word of God and the words of Scripture. One such expression is the concept of the indirect identity of the Word of God and Holy Scripture. Another is the concept of the brokenness or diffraction of revelation. Still another is the concept of Scripture as a witness to revelation.

If theologians deny this interval, then they must affirm that the words of Scripture in every instance perfectly mirror the Word of God. If there is no diastasis, then the interpreter is not allowed to make a difference between (1) those items in Scripture that are culturally bound to a given people, place, and time and (2) those elements that are transcultural and binding on all Christians everywhere. If there is no interval between the Word of God and the words of Scripture, then not one trace of an old world view can be allowed to stand in the text, for that would be approving an error. It also means that the accuracy of every biblical statement must be defended down to the last decimal point.

The truth of the matter is that historic and evangelical views of inspiration admit the diastasis. It is admitted when the genuine humanity of the Scripture is confessed, or when the concession is made that Scripture may speak at times in a very general or imprecise way, or when it is admitted that the weighing and measuring system of the Scriptures is not part of binding infallible revelation.

The difference between Barth and the historic view of inspiration is that Barth consciously builds the diastasis into his theology of revelation and inspiration so that matters of the humanity of Scripture are taken in stride. In the historic view, however, the diastasis is composed of all those nettling, disturbing aspects of Scripture ("the phenomena of Scripture") that hover distressingly at the edge of the theology of inspiration.

From such an analysis of Barth's diastasis, it is obvious he is working with the data of Scripture as such, and not intruding some Kantianism or some defective view of God's transcendence into his theology. One does not have to go to Kant or to a doctrine of divine transcendence to discover the diastasis or interval; one discovers it in the interpretation of the biblical text.

In his book *Evangelical Theology*, Barth makes the unusual statement that the Word of God is not immediately obvious "in any of its chapters or verses. On the contrary, the truth of the Word must be *sought*" (his italics).[3] That is because the diastasis in scripture exists and if the interpreter is not careful he or she may convert something of passing culture into the very Word of God itself. A good example is in Ephesians 2:2, where Satan is called "the prince of the power of the air." In Jewish thought, the *air* or *atmosphere* is the space that intervenes between the earth and God's throne. Some fundamentalists have taken the verse in an unimaginative literalism and have used it to criticize radio and television, which broadcast over "the airwaves." This concept of air or atmosphere is certainly not a part of scientific cosmology.

But notice that verb *sought*. The Word of God is to be *sought* in the text. Barth says this seeking is to be done by every means possible: philological and historical criticism, contextual relationships, and every device of conjectural imagination. By studying the text, the interpreter penetrates the diastasis to the

Word of God itself. As a matter of fact, that is precisely what evangelical interpreters do. In reading evangelical commentaries on Ephesians 2:2, we discover that they replace the words *air* or *atmosphere* with *spiritual;* that is, Satan's rule is not visible and "physical," but spiritual. The evangelicals have penetrated through the diastasis to the Word of God in the text.

As much as Barth may speak of this interval in Scripture, he does emphasize that the Word of God is on the other side of the interval. He specifically writes that the human and historical aspects of the writers do not detract from the fact that the authors of Scripture are objective, reliable witnesses of the Word of God.[4] The languages and culture of the authors may deflect the revelation of God from its original purity, but nevertheless the Word of God is in the text of Scripture. Those who deny that Barth teaches propositional revelation have not consistently followed Barth's understanding of Holy Scripture. Barth expresses the actual, objective revelation in the text of Scripture in the following three concepts.

1. *The concept of the* Bild. The German word *Bild* means "picture." The Word of God is in the text as a *Bild.* Because of the interval, the diastasis in the text, the Word of God is not obvious. The exegesis of the text brings out the *Bild,* which is then the Word of God in the text.

When Barth had to leave Germany under the ban of Hitler, he left as his advice to the Christians in Germany the words "Exegesis! Exegesis! Exegesis!" He meant that only by the exegesis of the biblical text could the Christians in Germany discover the Word of God and so understand Hitler and his program and have the will to fight it.

2. *The concept of* Sache. The German word *Sache* ordinarily means "thing," but when used of a piece of literature it means the burden or the substance or the meaning of the piece of literature. Barth believes that the Word of God is in Scripture as the *Sache* of Scripture. Just as it is the function of exegesis to uncover the *Bild* in Scripture, it is also the function of exegesis

to recover the *Sache* of the divine Word in Scripture.

3. *The concept of the* Wort *in the words.* This concept says the same thing about Scripture as is said by the concepts of *Bild* and *Sache*. Due to the interval between the text of Scripture and the Word of God, the words of Scripture are not immediately the Word of God. However, because Holy Scripture is inspired, the Word is in Scripture. This concept is expressed by saying that the Word is in the words, and good biblical interpretation will bring that Word to clarity.

In "The Hermeneutics of Karl Barth," Thomas Provence cites three other words as synonyms to the ones we have suggested: *das Gesagte,* "that which is said"; *das Bezeichnete,* "that which is described"; and *das Gegenstand,* "the object."[5] However, for clarity of exposition I will use the three mentioned in the preceding paragraphs.

This notion of *Bild, Sache,* and *Wort* shows that the key is the interpretation of Scripture. The revelation of God comes to humanity and is couched in human words with their linguistic and cultural mixing. The exegesis or interpretation of Scripture penetrates through the words to the *Bild, Sache,* and *Wort.*

Furthermore, Barth's notion of the Word of God being in the text of Scripture as *picture, substance,* and *word* (which can be discovered by proper biblical exegesis) means that Barth does not have the purely subjective, purely existential view of Scripture of which he is so frequently accused. There is an objective sense in which the Word of God is in Scripture, and many studies of Barth so concentrate on the proposed denials of Barth that the affirmations of Barth are left untouched.

The usual evangelical interpretation of Barth (even among some of the more academically oriented) is that his view of Scripture is subjective and existential. It is a kind of theological "now you see it, now you don't." I have referred already to the fact that Barth cites Scripture 15,000 times, in addition to 2,000 separate exegetical sections. No doubt some of these interpretations are very speculative, but that is not the point. The point is that Barth so views the objective authority of Scripture, and Scripture as the Word of God, that he cites it 15,000 times and makes 2,000 exegetical studies. If the proof of the pudding is in the eating, Barth has scored heavily. The question to be asked simply is "Do any evangelical or fundamentalist theologians reveal this much concentrated reference to Holy Scripture in their theology?"

Barth's concept of the diastasis enables a theologian to come to terms with modern learning and at the same time retain the theological integrity of Holy Scripture—which the doctrines of inspiration and revelation are really all about.

Barth's favorite designation of Holy Scripture is that it is a "witness to divine revelation." Because the expression is so systematically misunderstood, it is necessary to give a brief summary of the concept.

A witness in the biblical sense is one who participates in the event, which is the content of the witness. The witness is not the detached observer. The writers of Holy Scripture are participants in the experience of revelation, in the event of revelation, as well as recorders of it.

A witness is not any person, but a person elected by God to be a witness. The writers of Holy Scripture are, according to Barth, the most select of all human beings. They were elected to be the instruments for the writing of Holy Scripture.

A witness is a willing, active participant in the task of bearing witness. Barth's concept of inspiration focuses strongly on this point, but by defining it as the willingness to be a participant in the recording of revelation Barth prevents his theory of inspiration from being only that of poetic or artistic inspiration. The data are given to the witnesses; witnesses do not create, as do writers, painters, or composers.

A witness is assisted by the Holy Spirit. His or her witness is not solely that of his or her own powers but is everywhere enabled and inspired by the Holy Spirit.

The final and completed product of the witnessing is the written Word of God, which occurs in the church as Holy Scripture.

———◦◦———

The amount of materials in Barth's writings on the concept of the Word of God is very great, so only a listing of key ideas can be given here. First, the Word of God occurs in this world as Holy Scripture. Holy Scripture as the Word of God is the divine authority of God in this world and in the church. On this score, there is no difference between Barth and the strictest orthodox theologian.

Second, the Word of God is spiritual, which means that it is appropriated by spiritual means. It is a rational Word, which means that the human reason is involved in its appropriation. But as a spiritual Word something more is required, such as faith, meditation, prayer, and obedience. On the divine side, the Word is assisted by the Holy Spirit.

Third, people who are not Christians may read and understand Holy Scripture and books of Christian theology at the level of rational communication. Christian revelation is not in an odd language or composed of hidden or esoteric symbols. But the perception of the text of Scripture as the Word of God can be had only when, in addition to the rational criterion, spiritual criteria are used.

Fourth, the Word of God is dyadic or "two-term" in structure. This is the meaning of the Word of God as event. There must be a hearing that goes with the sermon, a hearing in faith. There must be faith in the reading of Scripture. Sometimes this event is described as encounter. The point is that the Word of God as something spiritual can be appropriated only in a spiritual way.

Calvin said that the divinity of Holy Scripture was evident in its majesty. Beyond the claim to inspiration, Scripture had to have a quality that was a witness to its divinity. This concept of the majesty of Scripture marking out its divinity has dropped out of the discussion in evangelical literature. As a student of Calvin, Barth retains it. This is another one of those many instances where Barth revives something from the period of the Reformation but in turn is accused of introducing something novel. The Word of God is detected in Scripture because of the majesty of its own nature. A lion is not only known by its anatomy to be a lion; it is also identified by the majesty of its roar.

This dyadic notion of the Word of God has been the basis for some evangelicals to affirm that Barth has a subjective view of the Word of God. However, to the given Word of God there must also be the spiritual response of a person, as affirmed by a long tradition from Augustine's illumination theory to Thomas's light of faith, to Luther's spiritual clarity of the Word of God, to Calvin's witness of the Spirit, to sections in orthodox dogmatics on the illumination of the Holy Spirit.

As noted, endless citations in *Church Dogmatics* indicate that Holy Scripture is the Word of God in the church and the final authority in matters of theology in the church. For example,

> We must at this point recall the basic rule of all Church dogmatics: that no single item of Christian doctrine is legitimately grounded, or rightly developed or expounded, unless it can of itself be understood and explained as a part of the responsibility laid upon the hearing and teaching Church towards the self-revelation of God attested in Holy Scripture.[6]

Part of the major strategy of Barth's theology is to reintroduce into theology the final authority of Holy Scripture after it had been denied by the Enlightenment and through the period of liberal Christianity. Yet he intends to make this reintroduction *into* our knowledge after the Enlightenment, not in defiance of the Enlightenment. That is why Barthian theology is so unpalatable to evangelicals who choose to ignore the Enlightenment and to liberal Christians who have capitulated to the Enlightenment.

First of all, Barth proclaims the *direct, absolute,* and *material* authority for Holy Scripture.[7] This affirmation is as strong as any that an orthodox or evangelical or fundamentalist person could make. So strong is Barth's stance on the sovereign authority of Holy Scripture in the church that he has been accused of "revelational positivism."

The label "revelational positivism" means that Barth believes everything taught in the Holy Scripture simply because it is written in Holy Scripture. The applicable German proverb is "Eat bird or die"; in English, it is "Like it or lump it." Barth does not believe he is a "revelational positivist," because he does take into account the historical-critical approach to Scripture. Nonetheless, the charge itself shows Barth's reputation among theologians for his exceptionally high regard for the final authority of Holy Scripture.

———◦∞◦———

Barth's strong stand for the supreme authority of Scripture in the church has frightened his fellow scholars and other theologians. I discuss Barth and humanism elsewhere, but wish to point out here that in the Geneva conference on humanism in 1949 Barth's speech on humanism was based on the authority of Scripture. The speech panicked the philosopher Jaspers into saying that Barth was attempting to put everybody under the tyranny of Holy Scripture. Barth knows, of course, that one cannot speak of the divine authority of Holy Scripture in the post-Enlightenment period as one could in the seventeenth century of Protestant scholasticism.

One of the most beautiful things Barth has written is the little booklet, *"Die Botschaft von der freien Gnade Gottes"* ("The Witness of the Free Grace of God"). Its basic thesis is that all of God's ways with humanity are marked by the fullness of divine grace. Barth places the matter of the authority of Scripture within the context of grace. The authority of Scripture is received by the believer within grace! It has not always been that way, but that is the way it must be in the post-Enlightenment period.

If there is a mistake in the older treatment of the authority of Scripture (which is also, unfortunately, current), it is to speak of obedience to the authority of Holy Scripture outside the context of grace and freedom. An authority legalistically imposed always undergoes the possibility of being rebelliously resisted. Authority within grace and freedom is an easy yoke to bear, and that is the kind of yoke Barth wants to put on post-Enlightenment people.

Barth's thesis can be summed up as follows: If a person comes to the authority of Holy Scripture within the context of grace, there is no conflict between freedom and authority. Authority accepted in grace produces joy, not resentment nor rebellion. Therefore, in a kind of paradoxical or dialectical mood, the Christian announces the full, sovereign material authority of Holy Scripture and at the same time announces that such an authority is to be received from the perspectives of divine grace and human freedom. Authority so internalized produces joy and happiness, not complaints, protests, and long faces.

How can Barth's theology be a paradigm in these matters? Current evangelical literature on the subject of inspiration does not know how to creatively handle the problem of the diastasis. On the one hand, it is clearly recognized when the humanity of Scripture is discussed, or the biblical language, or the obvious Hebrew culture of the Old Testament, or the Greco-Roman culture of the New Testament. The most common solution is to affirm that inspiration overcomes all these problems so they need not distress us. But this is no solution to the problem of the interval or diastasis.

As indicated earlier, Barth's understanding of the diastasis enables him to work it creatively into his theology. The diastasis is a necessary aspect of the process of revelation, not an unexpected embarrassment. If evangelicals do not approve of Barth's version of the diastasis then they must provide one that does much the same thing; that is, one that explains how a revelation given in and through an ancient culture can yet have a binding authority on peoples of other cultures and later centuries.

Barth knows that the concept of authority has been suspect among the children of the Enlightenment. He therefore comes to terms with the Enlightenment by presenting biblical authority under the umbrella of grace and freedom. Such a reception of authority brings with it its own joy without resentment. Calvin discovered in Geneva the ugly resentment bred by authority imposed without grace and freedom. The angry townspeople named their dogs Calvin. And the "moral majority" of recent years also has discovered the ugly resentment that graceless authoritarian morality generates. Psychiatrists also know that one root of criminality is parental authority without parental love. Barth's paradigm of authority under grace and freedom should be welcome to evangelicals.

Notes

1. Barth, *CD*, III/4, p. 328.
2. Barth, *CD*, II/1, p. 195.
3. Karl Barth, *Evangelical Theolgy: An Introduction*, trans. Grover Foley (New York: Holt, Rinehart & Winston, 1963), p. 35.
4. Barth, *CD*, III/3, p. 201.
5. Thomas Edward Provence, "The Hermeneutics of Karl Barth," unpublished doctoral dissertation, Fuller Theological Seminary, 1980, p. 145.
6. Barth, *CD*, II/2, p. 35.
7. Barth, *CD*, I/2, p. 538.

8

The Humanity of
Holy Scriptures

THEOLOGIANS HAVE AFFIRMED that Holy Scripture is at the same time a human and a divine book. It possesses both humanity and divinity. Biblical scholars in the period of the Enlightenment pointed out the humanity of Scripture especially in such a manner as to embarrass its divinity. If the history of biblical criticism from the Enlightenment to the present has been characterized by anything, it has been characterized by more and more revealing the humanity of Holy Scripture.

On the other hand, the history of theology shows how difficult it has been for both Roman Catholic and Protestant scholars to correlate properly the divinity and humanity of Holy Scripture (see Bruce Vawter's book, *Biblical Inspiration*). The problem is similar to the one in Heisenberg's Principle of Indeterminacy. The more the humanity of Scripture is emphasized, the more its divinity drifts out of focus; the more its divinity is emphasized, the more its humanity drifts out of focus. It does not seem possible to have simultaneous sharp images of the Scripture's humanity and divinity.

Any doctrine of Holy Scripture and its inspiration that does not come to the fullest, frankest, most honest confrontation with the full range of the humanity of Holy Scripture will certainly be written off as obscurantist.

———⁙———

As such a diligent student of the history of theology in the eighteenth, nineteenth, and twentieth centuries, Barth knows the whole story of the humanity of the Holy Scripture as well as the story of the biblical criticism of both Testaments. There is nothing new we can tell him about this history. The question is how Barth handles the problem of the humanity of the Holy Scripture.

Barth's solution is radically different from any of the ones usually offered. Barth believes we have to touch bottom on the matter of the humanity of Holy Scripture. We cannot in any way spare it. We must be prepared to gulp down whole the full, unabridged humanity of Holy Scripture.

With reference to its humanity, Holy Scripture is a totally human book. It is human in its languages and therefore reflects all the oddities of the Hebrew and Greek languages. Although it has been charged that current evangelical views about inspiration run contrary to the science of linguistics, this charge cannot be made against Barth. He lets the languages be the languages!

Furthermore, he lets the cultures be the cultures. Obviously, the Old Testament came to the Jewish people through many cultural periods. The biblical history painfully and accurately reflects these cultures. For example, the Scriptures use ancient measuring systems—for dry measurements, liquid measurements, distances, and weights. The marriage and burial customs were customs of the times. The relationships within the families were those of the prevailing cultures.

One of Barth's clearest statements on the humanity of Scripture is in his discussion of the creation account.[1] The record is to be read in its total humanity and not doctored or dressed up to make it read better. The vessel is of earth, and therefore all the marks of the earth will mark the vessel. It is a letter, a document, like all other letters, and does not have some magical property making it different from others. We are not to amend or improve or cover the nakedness of the text. It is entirely possible that where it seems the most human and the most vulnerable, it may be the strongest witness to the Word of God.*

When Barth was asked, in his appearance at the University of Chicago, if his admission of errors in Scripture "sullied" the divine authority of Scripture, Barth objected. He objected to the verb *sullied*. His argument was that if the Scriptures have a genuine humanity, then the presence of errors is part of the full humanity of the Scriptures and therefore does not sully the Scriptures. He also declared that, if God is not ashamed of errors in the Scripture, why should we be?[2] He also said that if we affirm the Scripture is without error because inspired by God, then God would be the cause of unbelief if we found errors in Scripture.

Evangelicals and Barth agree that one must affirm the humanity of Holy Scripture. The question is "How far is its humanity to be admitted?" Barth wants to hit bottom; that is, to affirm the full, unrestricted humanity of Scripture. This means that the writers of Scripture could err in their humanity. Evangelicals hedge the humanity of Scriptures by surrounding it with the divinity of Scripture. At least Barth wishes to make no half-hearted affirmation of the humanity of Scripture nor an affirmation of the humanity of Scripture that is undermined by an overpowering affirmation of its divinity.

--------◆◇◆--------

There are certain gains to Barth's doctrine of the humanity of the Scriptures. He does not have to defend all the patently human elements of Scripture as if they were an embarrassment to Scripture. He doesn't have to engage in all the tricks of harmonization to smooth out differences among the four Gos-

---

*Those who have read the works of the English theologian L. D. Thornton will recognize the close parallel of thought here between Thornton and Barth. Thornton argues that all of the features of the humiliation of the Son of God in the incarnation must also in their own way be true of revelation in the humiliated form of Holy Scripture. We are not to be embarrassed by the obvious humanity and earthiness of Scripture, but strengthened by them. Lionel D. Thornton, *Revelation and the Modern World* (London: Dacre Press, 1950).

pels. He doesn't have to argue in a sophisticated linguistic manner that the poor grammar of the Book of Revelation does not disqualify it as an inspired book of God. He doesn't have to postulate an inerrant original text in order to live at peace with the errant extant copies. He doesn't have to debate whether the trivial things of Scripture (the famous *levicula*, or "trivial things," in Scripture) are as divinely inspired and possibly have as great theological significance as the other material.

I don't think that Barth is primarily worried at this point about the baying dogs of the Enlightenment. I think he is working in parallel to the incarnation. In both the humanity of Christ and the humanity of Scripture, the theologian must touch bottom. One must affirm that the Son of God took actual sinful humanity in the incarnation and also that the Scriptures are vulnerable to error. In doing so, Barth is able to come to terms with the critical heritage of the Enlightenment and the current state of biblical studies. This is one reason why the children of the Enlightenment hear him, even though they may not agree with him.

Barth really touches bottom on the humanity of Holy Scripture when he says that there are errors in Holy Scripture, even theological errors. Granted, this statement has stirred up an angry response, but we ought to see what point Barth is making before his idea is rejected. The point is that at no place in our doctrine of Holy Scripture can we spare it from its full humanity. If to be human is to err, then it is a possibility that on the human side of Scripture there may be error. I don't recall that Barth anywhere says there *must be* error to be human (as I think Heinrich Vogel argues in *Gott in Christo*), but only as a matter of fact there is error.

Most evangelical treatises on inspiration follow the same strategy in dealing with the humanity of Scripture. Formally, the humanity of Scripture is fully granted. But then it is said that all the humanity of Scripture (such as the personalities of the authors) is part of the grand, providential strategy to prepare the writers of Scripture to write what they wrote. That there is truth in this notion is granted. It would be foolish to contest it. But the manner in which it is argued really negates the authentic humanity of Scripture. In other words, the humanity of Scripture is so protected by the divinity that in effect the humanity is greatly reduced.

Another facet of the manner in which traditional evangelical literature on inspiration undermines the humanity of Scripture is—at least in extreme statements—to totally reject any cultural conditioning of revelation. This rejection has the odd effect of making even biblical culture part of infallible revelation. In Christological language, this means that the manner in which evangelical literature on inspiration handles the humanity of Scripture is to more and more create a docetic Scripture (a view of Scripture in which the divinity of Scripture greatly diminishes the genuine, authentic necessary humanity of Scripture).

The stock charge against Barth at this point is that if he admits error into Scripture, then the revelation of God in Holy Scripture is confused. The Christian does not know then what is truth and what is error in Romans or John's Gospel. If error does not sully the Word of God, it certainly makes it impossible to know what is the truth of God in Scripture.

But, the critic of Barth affirms, if the full inerrancy of the text is affirmed then the problem ceases to exist. At every point the interpreter is dealing with inerrant assertions.

How, then, does Barth handle the problem of discerning truth from error in Holy Scripture? His answer is that this is done by a thorough exegesis of the text. When the interpreter has done a thorough, exacting task of examining the text, consulting all the commentaries and other specialized books, the text will stand before him or her exactly for what it is. Of course, this examination includes all those things Barth understands by theological interpretation, such as prayer, meditation, and imagination. Such an examination is, therefore, not the impossible task it is made out to be. After all, the affirmation that the text is inerrant does not mean that it yields an inerrant meaning to the fallible, human interpreter.

This last point needs further exploration. The charge against Barth is that if he admits errors in Scripture, then it is impossible for the interpreter to really know what is the truth of God in Scripture. But, as we pointed out, the affirmation of inerrancy does not ensure an inerrant interpretation of the text. Therefore, all evangelical interpreters of Scripture are caught in the mesh of having to make human, fallible decisions in interpreting Holy Scripture. The older Roman Catholic theology could appeal to infallible interpretations of an infallible revelation, but the Protestants have no such recourse.

First of all, there is the human decision about the canon. At present there are four different versions of the canon of the Old Testament, each resting on a human decision. The Lutheran and Reformed churches agree with the canon of the synagogue. The Roman Catholic Church accepts those extra books in the Old Testament Protestants call the Apocrypha. The Anglican Communion accepts the Apocrypha too, but only for purposes of edification and not for doctrine. The Eastern Orthodox Church accepts the Old Testament with Apocrypha in the Greek translation.

Second, there is the human decision about the text of Scripture. There is no divinely certified text of either the Old or New Testament. The science of textual criticism is a very human science, calling for hundreds of purely human decisions concerning which reading among the manuscripts is to be adopted.

Third, there is the human decision about how much of Old Testament revelation is binding on the Christian Church. This problem is obvious in the Christian debates over the Sabbath. Much historical reporting in Scripture is just there, and whether there is a Word of God for the Church in the sheer report is again a matter of human decision.

Finally, endless human decisions are involved in the interpretation of Scripture, wherein interpreters of equal loyalty to Holy Scripture arrive at different conclusions.

The doctrine of the inerrancy of Scripture does nothing to relieve the interpreter of Scripture from all these human decisions. To believe that Barth creates problems in his view of Scripture from which evangelicals are free is simply not the case. Every evangelical who interprets Scripture is caught in the web of decision making—human decision making. There are no divinely given answers to the questions of canon, text, and interpretation of Holy Scripture. It is a venture of grace and scholarship for all of us.

------◦◦◦------

The humanity of Scripture raises the question of biblical criticism. The fact that Barth does not accept the critical interpretation of the New Testament heart and soul came out in the debate over his commentary on the Book of Romans. In the preface, he wrote now-famous lines:

> The historical-critical method of Biblical investigation has its rightful place: it is concerned with the preparation of the intelligence—and this can never be superfluous. But, were I driven to choose between it and the venerable doctrine of Inspiration, I should without hestitation adopt the latter, which has a broader, deeper, and more important justification. Fortunately, I am not compelled to choose between the two.[3]

Barth's lifelong friend Thurneysen states Barth's view about biblical criticism as follows:

> Karl Barth has never denied the established findings of historical-critical research. He was happy with it because it set him free from the dogma of a false "positivism of revelation" [that is, everything in Scripture is believed on the simple basis that it is in Scripture]. But he did not let himself be free to the point that he would turn around and subject the biblical truth to a new liberal dogma of the validity of a current world view [by which the New Testament must be criticized]. He has made the effort to again earnestly perceive the voice of the biblical witnesses right through all "myths and legends" and to be sure, down to the last letter.[4]

Here again we see why it is so difficult to get Barth into proper focus. At the same time, he accepts the established results of biblical criticism and affirms the full theological integrity of Holy Scripture. He rejects the stance of his own theological teachers, who believed that the critical study of Scripture implied the destruction of its theological integrity. We have seen that this was already done by the Neologians of the Enlightenment and that the liberal Christianity of the nineteenth and twentieth centuries have followed the Neologians.

This position of Barth's came to the surface in the famous exchange of letters, in the German periodical *Christian World*, between Harnack and Barth (a story in itself!). Harnack was the leading theologian of liberal Christianity, and in his letters he defended the typical liberal stance that the scientific interpretation of Scripture put an end to the orthodox understanding of Holy Scripture. Barth countered by saying that he had no objections to modern scientific learning, but on the other hand the Word of God in Holy Scripture was greater than that!

Barth divides the house! He will not adopt the older union of the theological integrity of Scriptures and the older traditional and conservative views in matters of biblical introduction. Nor will he, with liberal Christians, affirm that the critical study of Scripture undermines its theological integrity. He goes a narrow, lonely way in affirming the basic validity of modern critical methods and at the same time affirming the complete theological integrity of Holy Scripture.

It is because Barth has a dualistic or split-ticket approach to Scripture that James A. Wharton finds it difficult to get Barth into focus.[5] Wharton sees quite clearly that Barth follows both a critical and a theological approach to scripture, but how Barth got there and how he operates with the two methods drifts out of focus. Only when one sees Barth as a child of the Enlightenment (who accepts biblical criticism) and a critic of the Enlightenment (who maintains the historic faith of the church in the theological integrity of Scripture) does his position begin to drift back into focus.

I have summed up Barth's general stance toward criticism in five theses, as follows:

First, *the inspired canonical book is the final edition of it.* The Pentateuch as it now stands is the Word of God. It may have taken ten sources and five rewrites, but that has nothing to do with its final form. The inspired, canonical status of Daniel is not threatened if it took two Daniels to write it—an earlier Daniel for the earlier chapters and a later Daniel for the final chapters. The composite or edited nature of a book of the Scriptures does not militate against its inspiration nor its canonical status.

Second, *the truth is in the text regardless of critical issues.* Barth agrees that the backdrop of Genesis 1–3 could well be mythological Babylonian creation stories. And further, he admits the large gap in world views between Genesis 1 and Genesis 2–3. However, each is its own theological witness, and each is to be heard as a theological witness. It is not mandatory to follow either the orthodox tradition and try to harmonize the accounts or the critical tradition, which sees only conflict in the two accounts.

Barth's attitude is the same with reference to the resurrection accounts. The accounts are human witnesses, and, as with all human witnessing, when there are two or more witnesses, the accounts are jumbled. There is neither sense nor need to work out a harmony of the resurrection appearances. The texts do bear witness to the bodily resurrection of Jesus Christ.

Third, *the biblical texts are witnessing texts, not sources for the critical reconstruction of history.* It has become a common assumption among both Old and New Testament specialists that the real story is the history reconstructed behind biblical history. Barth objects. This approach turns Scripture into a book of sources (*Quellensammlung, Quellenliteratur*). According to the critical method, the real history of Israel is the reconstructed history of Israel; the real Jesus is the Jesus reconstructed behind the texts; and the real history of the Book of Acts is the story of the church as retold by historical reconstruction.

To treat the Scriptures as a sourcebook is a fundamental violation of the most basic principle of interpretation: *a book is to be interpreted in the light of what it claims to be.* The Holy Scripture claims to be a book of witnesses to the revelation of God. Therefore to interpret them as sources and not witnesses is to blunder at the point of fundamental theory of interpretation.

If a scholar tells us another history other than that recorded of the church in the Book of Acts, it may be history but it has lost its character as a witness to revelation. Historical reconstructions are not witnesses to revelation. Only Holy Scripture, as it stands, without reconstruction, is the primal witness to revelation.

This position is the reason why Barth has never endorsed the quest for the historical Jesus. The quest implies that there is another Jesus behind the Gospels. If there is such a Jesus, it is not the Jesus of the Gospels as they now stand. Barth asks why this reconstructed Jesus is always such a pale Jesus. Certainly the Jesus that emerges from the "criteria of authenticity" is a very pale, even anemic Jesus!

The one assertion that Barth will not negotiate is that the text of Scripture as it stands is a witness to revelation, and must be read, understood, and interpreted as a witness to revelation. As soon as the text is converted into any kind of source document with the real history or the real meaning behind the text as it stands, then Scripture is betrayed. Because Barth stands so solidly and resolutely on this affirmation, he is out of step with virtually all Old and New Testament scholars whose daily work is based on the presupposition that Holy Scripture is basically a source document and not the primeval document of divine revelation.

Fourth, *the historical-critical method of interpretation is a necessary but preliminary method that cannot give the meaning of the text.* Or, to put it positively, only the theological interpretation of the text gets to its meaning.

Critical commentaries are filled with notes on the Hebrew or Greek languages. They also usually contain geographical, historical, and cultural references. If the text calls for it, there is discussion of textual criticism. Barth approves of all this but also insists that none of this explains the text. Such methods do not yield the meaning of the text. In his booklet *Das Geschenk der Freiheit*, Barth contrasts the analytic method of treating Scripture (the historical-critical) with the synthetic method (the theological). One weakness of the analytical method is that about every thirty years another New Testament guru pulls it away in another direction. The basic weakness of the method is that it does not get to the meaning of the text. The quest for meaning is the task of the synthetic or theological method, which in principle includes listening to the text, meditation, and prayer. Barth urges that both methods must be carried on at the same time, but with the provision that one should never confuse (1) technical details found in a critical commentary with (2) the exposition of the text in search of its meaning.

Of course, Barth is neither loved nor followed by Old or New Testament scholars. The specialists are too wedded to the technicalities of their specialization. Barth's reply to them is that over a hundred years or so it will be decided whether his method or the limited historical-critical really does justice to the text and meaning of Scripture.

This conflict can be seen very clearly in the Christological studies of such New Testament experts as Rudolph Bultmann, Ernst Käsemann, Willi Marxsen, and those scholars in England and America who follow their methodology. Form criticism, redaction criticism, and source criticism all presuppose that the reconstructed story is the real story and that the Gospels serve only as sources.

Barth may not object to any of these methods if they aid in the understanding of the Gospels. He has expressed his doubts that the historical-critical method can truly evoke the meaning of the text. However, the Christian church is bound to the witness of the Gospels as they are written, not to the story as reconstructed.

Certainly the reconstruction is not a simple procedure of going behind the texts to find the real story. Current studies presume a very powerful Hellenistic influence on New Testament writers; in fact, so powerful that they could not escape formulating most of their leading ideas in the language of Hellenistic religious terminology. To put it another way, exegesis has become research in the contemporary society of the New

Testament writers. The concepts as used in the Hellenistic culture are their meanings in the New Testament. A typical example of this is James Dunn's *Christology in the Making*, in which the social-religious-cultural grid sets the limits on what the New Testament may say about the incarnation. Cultural research in terminology replaces exegesis. Barth knows the outlines of current New Testament studies and chooses to go his own lonely way in biblical studies.

Fifth, *Barth rejects content* (Sache) *criticism*. Rudolph Bultmann contended that the message of the New Testament was infiltrated by Hellenistic myths and concepts and world views that could not be believed by modern people. The Hellenistic culture at the time of the writing of the New Testament contaminated the message. Hence those elements that contaminate the message must be located and retranslated (demythologized) into our modern acceptable existential concepts. This approach is known as "content criticism," or *Sachkritik*. To be very specific, the New Testament does teach the incarnation, the vicarious death of Christ, and the bodily resurrection. But modern New Testament scholars who know their mythology and demythologizing are not bound to believe such New Testament teachings. They have the right to pursue content criticism.

Although Barth admits the cultural diastasis in Holy Scripture, he never sees it as creating the contamination or distortion that Bultmann affirms. Hence Barth rejects content criticism. Barth's stance is that once we have done our critical homework and determined the meaning of Holy Scripture (such as the affirmation of an incarnation), then in good Christian conscience we are bound to believe it.

Barth therefore parts company with the whole movement in modern New Testament studies that works on the premise that the whole Christology (save for a few shreds!) of the New Testament is phrased in Hellenistic myths or mythological concepts and therefore must be drastically "retooled" for modern Christian people.

In the recent spate of evangelical essays on inspiration, it is apparent that the humanity of Scripture is proving difficult to harmonize with the theory of inspiration being proposed. Older solutions are repeated with a flourish of some more recent learning. But the essayists sturdily refuse to grant that the modern sciences of linguistics, anthropology, and historical research are any cause to rethink the humanity of Scripture. In such essays, the humanity of Scripture is so carefully encased in its divinity that the humanity of the Scriptures is not allowed to speak for itself.

The presupposition at work here is that if the humanity of Scripture is fully granted, then all will be lost. The hole in the dike will become larger and larger until it cannot be plugged. The strategy must be, then, to stop the process before it begins.

However, putting such a tight lid on the humanity of Scripture creates other problems. It can only be done by the policy of obscurantism; namely, anything about Scripture as a book or the composition of Scripture or the nature of Scripture that is addressed by modern learning must be in principle denied because its admission would ruin the theory.

This problem comes most clearly to focus with reference to biblical criticism. It is in criticism that the humanity of Scripture is dealt with most exclusively. Evangelicals grant the right and necessity of biblical criticism, but only in a very guarded and limited fashion. All adverse criticism is dismissed for such reasons as (1) the proponents of "higher criticism" have philosophical presuppositions that lead them inevitably to a distortion in their interpretation of the facts. (2) The proponents of adverse criticism may also have theological opinions such as liberalism, existentialism, or antisupernaturalism, which cause them to distort the interpretation of the facts. Or (3) critical theories come and go with a rapidity suggesting that the subjective factors far outweigh the objective factors in their interpretation.

There is enough truth in these assertions to make the beginnings of a case. The weakness of such a stance is that much material is totally independent of all these factors and with which evangelicals must therefore come to terms. Otherwise they are open to the charge of obscurantism. The Synoptic Problem is just there, regardless of anybody's philosophy or theology as are all the problems created by John's Gospel in its variations from the Synoptic Gospels. Paul's letters come in three distinctive chunks: the "authentic" ones, the prison epistles, and the pastoral epistles. The Greek used in II Peter is very different from that of I Peter, and the relationship of II Peter to Jude is very obscure.

The above instances do not even scratch the surface. For almost every book of Holy Scripture raises serious, valid, and critical questions about its composition and authenticity that are totally independent of any theological or philosophical presuppositions.

But all this is secondary to the primary problem: *there is no genuine, valid working hypothesis for most evangelicals to interact with the humanity of Scripture in general and biblical criticism in particular.* There are only ad hoc or desultory attempts to resolve particular problems.

Barth's method of coming to terms with the humanity of the Scripture and biblical criticism is at least a clearly stated program. It enables him to deal with the humanity of Scripture in a full, free, open, nonobscurantist way. His method is a paradigm for how an evangelical can come to terms with the Enlightenment and the modern learning it has produced in historical science, linguistics, and anthropology, and yet retain the full theological integrity of Holy Scripture. To date, evangelicals have not announced such a clear working program. If Barth's paradigm does not please them, they are still under obligation to propose a program that does enable an evangelical to live creatively with evangelical theology and biblical criticism. Only by such a program can evangelicals exorcize the evil demon of obscurantism.

Notes

1. Barth, *CD*, III/1, pp. 93–94.
2. Barth, *CD*, I/2, p. 531.
3. Karl Barth, *The Epistle to the Romans*, trans. Edwyn C. Hoskyns (Oxford, England: Oxford University Press, 1933), p. 1.
4. Eduard Thurneysen, in *Antwort*, p. 836.
5. James A. Wharton, in "Karl Barth as Exegate in His Influence on Biblical Interpretation," *Union Seminary Quarterly Review* 28 (Fall 1972), pp. 15–30.

9

The Divinity of
Holy Scriptures

THE NEOLOGIANS and biblical critics of the Enlightenment did much to destroy the historic Christian belief in the divine origin of Holy Scripture. By pointing out the very human characteristics of Holy Scripture, they intended to deny the possibility of its divinity. Again, Barth knows this story but refuses to concede to either the Neologians or the biblical critics.

Just as Barth confesses the full humanity of Scripture, he confesses the full divinity of Scripture. Most evangelicals doubt this, so I here cite some of Barth's statements and indicate the German words used. The Scripture is the Word of God because its witness, its content as divine revelation is *massgeblich*, or "authoritative," "normative," "standard";[1] *untrüglich*, "unerring," "infallible," "certain," "sure," "unmistakable";[2] and *unfehlbar*, or "unfailing," "infallible," "unerring."[3] In his *Evangelical Theology*, he uses three words in a row: *authentische*, "authentic"; *glaubwürdige*, "worthy of belief," "credible," "authentic"; and *authoritative*, "authoritative."[4]

His principal treatment of Scripture is in *Church Dogmatics I/2*, but statements about Scripture occur in all his volumes, and those need to be read too.

Barth's citation of Scripture is the most extensive in the

whole history of theology. Like Luther and Calvin, he had a detailed knowledge of Scripture short only of memorizing the text. Once when I visited him at Basel, I was admitted into his study before he came in. On his desk (kept so neat!) was a piece of paper, a pen, and a German and a Greek New Testament. On inspecting the paper, I discovered that he was making a concordance of verses on some topic. This was no surprise, for such listings of verses on a given topic occur all through the *Church Dogmatics*. In addition to such collections of verses, there are long exegetical passages in the *Church Dogmatics*. Barth's extensive knowledge of Scripture and use of Scripture reflects his profound belief in its divinity. As noted often before, *Church Dogmatics* contains about 15,000 biblical references and 2,000 separate exegetical passages. In fact, some have been printed in a separate volume because they were judged so valuable for a wider readership. Unfortunately, people whose reading of Barth is restricted to secondary sources have no idea of Barth's immense knowledge of Holy Scripture, his reverence for the text, and the theological value of the text that all such things imply. How cheap, then, to dismiss Barth in one sentence as an existential theologian!

--------⋖∞⋗--------

In the simplest statement possible, Barth believes in the divinity of Holy Scripture because it is a product of divine revelation. His motto is *"Revelation generates Scripture."* God moves in our space, in our time, in our history, to specific people (prophets and apostles) and so reveals himself and his purposes. Out of this self-revelation of God in our midst issues the witness to that revelation, which on being written down forms the Holy Scripture. This position denies any purely natural, purely human accounting for the origin of Holy Scripture.

This position means that Holy Scripture came into existence by divine inspiration, and that inspiration too is part of the divinity of Holy Scripture. Barth's version of the divine inspiration of Holy Scripture differs on two scores from much current evangelical opinion. First, evangelicals understand their version of the inspiration of Holy Scripture to be "church doc-trine." This view of inspiration has been held "everywhere, always, and by all" (*Vincentian Canon*). Barth understands the evangelical and fundamentalist version of inspiration to be a specific historic development out of religious conditions pre-vailing in the seventeenth and eighteenth centuries. Second, the doctrine of verbal inspiration and inerrancy represents a *materialization* of the doctrine of inspiration. By "materializa-tion" is meant that the Word of God is reduced literally to a book that one can carry around in one's pocket. The Word of God in its spiritual dimension has been lost.

It is reported that one professor of the Barthian persuasion placed a Bible on the platform in his lecture hall and then jumped up and down on it. No person can ever so treat the original, pure Word of God. One may jump on the witness of the Word of God, just as one can make martyrs of prophets and apostles. A doctrine of inspiration that leads to the materi-alization of the Word of God would permit a person to jump up and down on the Word of God. The wicked king in the book of Jeremiah could cut up the words of Jeremiah and burn them in the fire (Jeremiah 36), but only because they were Jeremiah's witness to the Word of God and not the Word of God itself.

However, this position does not mean that Barth has a sub-jective or existential view of divine inspiration. Barth's lectures at the Divinity School of the University of Chicago were re-corded and published by Word Record. One, then, can hear the actual voice of Barth in English on the matter of inspira-tion. In the question period he was asked, "Is not the objective character of the inspiration and normative function of the Bible impaired when the assumption is made that the Bible is sullied by inconsistencies and errors? How can a fallible Bible be the objective Word of God?"[5] I comment more extensively on the answer to this question elsewhere, but here I note that Barth replied he has always stressed the objective character of inspiration. Barth thus in his own words denies that his view of Holy Scripture is subjective or existential.

In a seminar in Basel (November 20, 1957), Barth affirmed that the Scripture could never be made into the Word of God by the force of our own listening. He also denied this subjectivistic interpretation of Scripture as the Word of God in his *Church Dogmatics.*[6]

Barth has always appealed to Luther's great doctrine of the Holy Spirit, and especially to Calvin's famous doctrine of the internal witness of the Holy Spirit, and would remind his orthodox and evangelical critics that he is just reviving Reformation doctrine.

In a personal interview with Barth (April 26, 1958), I put the following question to him as plainly and emphatically as I could: "Is not your view of revelation and inspiration so subjective that there are no theological propositions in Holy Scripture, hence the writing of theology is impossible?" His answer was that we do not have the pure Word of God in Scripture because it is already in the Hebrew or Greek language. The Word of God that the prophets and apostles did hear they did write down as witnessing records, which form the book we call Holy Scripture. The theological content in the original Word of God is, however, carried over into the written witness. Therefore there is a theological content in Holy Scripture, which is the basis of writing Christian theology.

In my last personal interview with Barth (July 11, 1958), I asked him is he still adhered to *Sache* exegesis (that is, did he still believe that there was a revelational substance in Scripture that was the task of the interpreter to discover?). He answered that he did.

In view of these interviews and the hundreds of similar pages in the *Church Dogmatics*, it is clear that Barth believes in both an objective doctrine of the divine inspiration of Scripture and a propositional element in revelation. It is therefore wrong to persist in affirming that Barth's doctrine of inspiration is totally subjective and that he denies propositional revelation.

To repeat, people who think that the only options about Holy Scripture are the ones of liberal Christianity or of traditional orthodox Christianity have trouble getting Barth into focus. He appears to them as neither fish nor fowl, so he must be covertly a neomodernist. But Barth is surely splitting the ticket by affirming all that the older doctrine of inspiration wishes to assert yet by so framing his doctrine of Scripture so as to come to terms with modern learning, biblical and otherwise.

No concept in Barth's theology has been criticized more than his concept of Scripture becoming the Word of God. The basic reason for this concept is twofold. The first is that Barth wishes to preserve the spirituality of the Word of God. By the spirituality of the Word of God, Barth means that the Word of God is recognized as such only under such spiritual conditions as faith, trust, obedience, prayer, and meditation. The concept is misunderstood if it is interpreted to mean that the Scripture in itself is not the Word of God but under certain conditions magically becomes the Word of God. The truth of the matter is that one may hear Barth's point made over and over again in the most fundamentalist of pulpits; namely, that God's Word is only heard as God's Word in penitence, faith, and obedience.

Barth does believe that Holy Scripture is the Word of God in itself. There is a continuous line from God to God in the act of revelation to the witnesses of revelation to the written witness we call Holy Scripture. However, for the Word of God to be recognized as the Word of God, spiritual prerequisites are necessary. In fulfilling these prerequisites, the Scripture then truly appears (becomes) as the Word of God to the believing heart. Barth did not invent this notion, for one can find it everywhere in the writings of the revelation and as far back as Augustine's doctrine of divine illumination. One can also find Barth's notion in the older theological works under the title of "The Divine Illumination of Holy Scripture."

Barth's second justification for his concept of Scripture becoming the Word of God has to do with the function of Holy Scripture in the Christian church. The orthodox view, especially as developed in the seventeenth century, was that Scripture is something like a set of legal cases in the lawyer's typical library. For specific cases of law, lawyers reach into their libraries for precedents. Such a view of Holy Scripture robs it of its power to ever again keep speaking anew to the church. Holy Scripture and the Word of God are dynamic, not static, entities. Scripture lives in the church and with the church, and is ever heard afresh. In the sense of ever speaking anew the Word of God to the church, Scripture becomes the Word of God.

Barth frames the Word of God in a threefold time dimension. First, it is a matter of experience that the Scriptures have in the past history of the church broken forth anew as the Word of God. Second, it is also a matter of experience that every Lord's Day, in numerous congregations, Holy Scripture is heard as the Word of God. Third, it is also a promise of Holy Scripture that it will in the future be heard as the Word of God. It is in this context that one must further understand Barth's concept of Scripture becoming the Word of God.

Barth's insistence on the spirituality of all things is a pervasive theme in his theology. He derives it from Calvin, who said that obedience is the beginning of all true knowledge of God. The Word of God is known as the Word of God only in obedience, not in apologetics. Barth prefers to call dogmas *Befehlen*—behests! They are more commands to be obeyed than dogmas to be rationally assimilated. Barth abhors the distinction between theory and practice, on the grounds that sinners will admit the theory and deny the practice. His doctrine of inspiration is thus formed to preserve the spirituality of the Word of God. To note that Barth differs form such great ones in the theory of inspiration as Louis Gaussen or Benjamin Warfield or Charles Hodge does not really come to terms with Barth's doctrine.

Barth does not have a condescending attitude toward the older doctrine of inspiration. Once he wrote that, if he had to choose between it and modern critical theories of the Scripture, he would choose the older view of the inspiration of Scriptures. Whatever its propounders may lack according to modern scholars, they did have a sound concept of the nature of Christian theology. Nor does Barth write off verbal inspiration. He suggests a substitute expression: *the verbalness of inspiration.* Revelation must be in words. Barth did not believe in revelation in the form of pictures, frescoes, statues, music, or dance; he believed that the precision we need in theology can only be had in words. Although he was opposed to the older doctrine of verbal inspiration, he did not deny that revelation must be in verbal form.

In Barth's review of the doctrinal history of the scriptural inspiration, he is not fundamentally opposed to the various high attributes given to Scripture. One must defend its supreme authority, its sufficiency, its verbal character, the divine in-breathing, and its absolute dependability. But he is opposed to so treating or defining these attributes as to rob Scripture of its power as the Word of God and to reduce Scripture to a casebook for settling theological debates. Such treatment or definition does not leave open the possibility that God can again and again speak his Word in the church through the Scripture. One may overprotect the Scripture as the Word of God, and in so doing close off that potential of Scripture for being the ever-living Word of God in the church. That is Barth's difference with the view of inspiration as developed especially in the seventeenth century. In short, the older view of inspiration *materializes* the Holy Scripture, and in so materializing it robbed Scripture of its *spiritual* and *dynamic* qualities, which enable it ever anew to speak the Word of God in the church.

I have explored, in Barth's theology of preaching, that moment of transition: "How do the human words of the preacher become the Word of God to the listener?" This issue is identical to the topic now under discussion: "How do the human words of Scripture *transit* into the Word of God and thence to the reader?" The elements in Barth's explanation are as follows:

1. *The grace of God.* Only through God, acting in his freedom and in his grace, can the transition take place. One reason why Barth speaks of the leap of faith is that faith always occurs in the context of grace. That distance between God and persons can only be bridged by grace! And thus faith can neither be controlled by human beings nor totally understood by human beings.

2. *The Holy Spirit.* In the light of historical theology, Barth is only restating in his own way Luther's doctrine of the spiritual clarity of Scripture and Calvin's doctrine of the internal witness of the Holy Spirit. In his famous theological treatise *The Bondage of the Will,* Luther defended the twofold thesis that the Scriptures were understood on a linguistic or grammatical basis and by the illumination of the Holy Spirit. Calvin set the pace for Reformed, Lutheran, and even Anglican theology in the *Institutes of the Christian Religion* in his famous chapter on the internal or secret witness of the Holy Spirit.[7]

3. *A mystery.* The mystery of the transition is like the imagery of the resurrected Christ going through closed doors. The moment of transition from the human words to the Divine Word of Scripture that takes place in the heart or spirit of the person is beyond any human analysis or introspection. In this sense, it is a mystery. It is something that truly happens but it is also beyond explanation.

These concepts of grace, the Holy Spirit, and mystery preserve the spirituality of the Word of God. That is to say, the divine Word in Scripture can be known and recognized only under spiritual considerations or only in a spiritual context.

Of course, some evangelicals suspect that there is something irrational in all this. In an interview with Barth (April 28, 1958), I put the following question to him as strongly and clearly as I could: "Do you challenge the law of contradiction and can you therefore not write a consistent dogmatics?"

His answer was that the subject matter of investigation determined the logic of the investigation. In theology, the nature of Christian theology determines the use of logic. If there were any tension between the law of contradiction and some point in divine revelation, then the law of contradiction has to yield.

Then he commented that only rarely, here and there in his dogmatics, did he feel conflict between his theology and logic. John Godsey also records Barth's rejection of irrationalism in theology, and his trust in reason as far reason can be followed. Reason is a good gift of God, but it is unreasonable to perceive our reason as greater than our God—the cardinal sin and mistake of the Neologians of the Enlightenment.[8] In his *Church Dogmatics,* Barth always stresses that revelation is a reasonable event. To represent him as wallowing in the paradoxical and irrational is true neither of the man nor of his theology. Barth could hardly make this point clearer than in the following words (italics added): "*Credo quia absurdum* (I believe [in Christianity] because it is absurd) would be the last thing to profit its object or to be permitted theology. *On the contrary, the theologian cannot possess, maintain, and demonstrate enough reason.*"[9]

This citation is worthy of special notice because it was spoken by Barth at the very end of his academic career, and he was speaking popularly but right to the point. He was declaring his opinions for certain and setting the record straight: "The theologian cannot possess, maintain, and demonstrate enough reason."

Barth's view of the Word of God as related to Holy Scripture does have some advantages and certainly has points on which evangelicals might reflect.

1. Barth has a clear doctrine on how the text of Scripture becomes the Word of God to the believing heart. The doctrine keeps the experience spiritual and thereby avoids magical and other views that have characterized some evangelical views of Scripture.

2. Barth is able to come to terms in a creative manner with the Scriptures, being at the same time human words and the Word of God. His version of the relationship does not call for endless apologetic sortees into science or history or biblical criticism in order to shore up Scripture.

3. Barth keeps the issues theological and therefore does not

attempt to give psychological or philosophical explanations of revelation and inspiration. He knows much more of the general area of the humanities than his *Dogmatics* suggests. His whole life, public and private, was lived among scholars, psychiatrists, physicians, and psychologists.

4. Barth's honesty with "the facts of the case," whatever the case might be, enables him to avoid the fateful blunder of obscurantism. He neither bluffs nor obscures but sets out the issues with a remarkable honesty.

Notes

1. Barth, *CD*, III/4, p. 7.
2. Barth, *CD*, III/1, p. 23.
3. Barth, *CD*, II/2, p. 633.
4. Karl Barth, *Evangelical Theology: An Introduction*, trans. Grover Foley (New York: Holt, Rinehart & Winston, 1963), p. 36.
5. Karl Barth, *Evangelical Theology* records 3231-3237 (Waco, Tex.: Word Records, 1962).
6. Barth, *CD*, I/2, pp. 534-535.
7. John Calvin, *Institutes of the Christian Religion*, trans. Ford Lewis Battles (Philadelphia: Westminster Press, 1960), Vol. I, Bk. I, chap. 7.
8. John Godsey, *Karl Barth's Table Talk* (Richmond, Va.: John Knox Press, 1962), p. 31.
9. Barth, *Evangelical Theology*, p. 92.

10

The Christological Scriptures

THE ENLIGHTENMENT SCHOLARS commented on the theological diversity within the Christian church and on the plurality of world religions. The great philosopher Gottfried Wilhelm Leibniz (1646–1716) made his own proposal to unify Christendom and heal its rifts. Lessing wrote his famous play *Nathan the Wise* to end competition among world religions. Theologians who propounded the truth of their own system were embarrassed by the need to confess that it was but one among competing options in the church.

The problem of religious pluralism raised in a faltering way by the Enlightenment has become intensified in the twentieth century. The Scriptures themselves are declared a pluralistic book, in that neither Old or New Testament scholars can agree on the common theme that unifies both Testaments. The Bible is really a diverse library—in Greek, *ta biblia*, "the books"—rather than a unified volume. Such books as James Dunn's *Unity and Diversity in the New Testament* pose embarrassing questions for traditional dogmatics. With such confessed pluralism in Scripture itself, and the pluralism of theologies to which the Scriptures give birth, is the Bible really a believable book for modern people?

————∞————

Barth boldly pronounces that the unity of the Holy Scripture and of Christian theology is Jesus Christ. This concept is not original with Barth, but it is true that Barth applies the thesis with ruthless consistency.

Augustine and the whole early church had affirmed that the New Testament lay hidden in the Old Testament, and that the Old became clear in the New. Its allegorical interpretation was essentially a Christological interpretation of all Scripture. Luther is famous for his remarks about the Christological character of Holy Scripture, and Calvin said that Christ is the mediator of all divine revelation. One even finds in fundamentalist literature an effort to find Christ in every single book of the Holy Scripture.

Barth's rationale for his Christological principle is that the highest point of revelation governs the whole history of revelation. The highest point is the incarnation as affirmed in John 1:14. Therefore Christian interpreters have as much right to look backward Christologically into the Old Testament as they have the right to look forward to the Christological passages in the epistles. Barth has also argued that the preexistence of Christ involves Christ's participation in the revelation of the Old Testament. Therefore Barth claims that it is not artificial for him to find Christ in the Old Testament, contrary to most Old Testament scholars.

Barth defends his Christological principle by indicating the dilemma of the rabbis who deny the Christological interpretation of the Old Testament. Barth essentially asks, "Where is the Old Testament going?" It is going somewhere, for it is filled with apocalyptic and eschatological materials. It has many visions of the future. A rabbi who denies that the Old Testament is going somewhere must systematically ignore all visions, dreams, apocalypses, and eschatological passages in the Old Testament. This denial makes the Old Testament resemble a dismembered torso, a road system halfway built and going nowhere, or a complex freeway interchange without any ramps leading to or away.

When Barth unifies the Holy Scripture with his Christological principle, he is not announcing a Christological system. He is not offering a plan or a schema whereby all all the different parts can be harmoniously adjusted to each other. Rather, what he suggests is more like a unifying theme, like the plot of an involved novel; the reader is not sure how all the parts of the novel fit together, yet knows what the novel is all about.

––––––––⟨∞⟩––––––––

The history of theology has been the history of the search for a theological concept that would harmonize Scripture and theology. The first great attempt was the recapitulation theology of Irenaeus (A.D. 130–200). Since then there have been such alternative systems as that of Thomas Aquinas, Lutheran theology, Reformed theology, salvation history, and dispensationalism.

Barth's Christological unity of scripture and theology is a bold attempt to cut this particular Gordian knot. His attempt is much more a procedural rule than a system. In fact, Barth denies the possibility of a systematic theology in the sense of a really systematized set of beliefs. The Scripture is a witness to God's revelation, and the witness is either too rich or too diversified or too miscellaneous to be able to be cast into systematic form. But in the Christological principle there is a unity of procedure. The function of the theologian is not to create a system but to follow the Christological principle in the witness of Holy Scripture. Viewed this way, Barth's theology is not distressed by the diversity of Scripture, or by a plurality of theologies in the New Testament or by any failure to totally systematize the teaching of Scripture (which, of course, has never been done). But he does insist that we can make sense out of Scripture and theology if the Christological premise is followed as the procedural rule in the writing of theology.

Barth's theology is, then, Reformed without being typically Calvinistic; it is deeply indebted to Luther (whom he cites more than any other theologian) without being Lutheran. It has deep roots in historical theology without being Roman Catholic. It is an effort to rewrite historic Christian theology without attaching itself too firmly to any of the historic options, although his sympathies are clearly with Calvin and the Reformed tradition. However, many of his favored Reformed positions are given a new Christological interpretation (e.g., election).

There are many similarities in Barth's methodology to Heinrich Vogel's methodology in *Gott in Christo*. Vogel's book is more than a thousand pages of theology, all governed by an intense Christological principle. Vogel and Barth were friends, and Vogel exerted some influence on Barth. If there were a paradigm of a theology in which all is written from a concentrated Christological stance, it would be Vogel's book.

Although the early church understood the Old Testament to be a Christian book (in that it foretold of Christ), the early church heretic Marcion was the exception. Marcion did not believe that the God of the Old Testament was the same person as the Father of the New Testament. Hence he split the Old Testament off from the New. The repudiation of the Old Testament as a Christological book is hence known as Marcionism.

Marcionism has been a powerful influence in theology since the nineteenth century. The radical criticism of that time would not allow anything supernatural in the Old Testament. There can be a witness to Christ in the Old Testament only if supernatural revelation exists. To deny supernatural revelation is to deny that any Old Testament writer could write of Jesus Christ; to deny that such a writer could anticipate Christ is to deny that the Old Testament is a Christological book. And that is Marcionism.

At this point the radical Protestants came very close to the Jewish view of the Old Testament; namely, that its merit rested in its monotheistic concept of God, its high ethical codes, and the spiritual life it sets before the true believer.

Marcionism still prevails in Old Testament studies. But it has precipitated a theological debate, for the whole history of the Christian church is built on the unity of the Testaments. Bultmann, a leading New Testament scholar of existentialist theology, barely saves the Old Testament by making it a book of humanity's existential failure as the preparation for the existential success story of the New Testament.

Into this battle-scarred territory comes Barth, reaffirming powerfully and radically the historic stance of the Christian church that the Old Testament is a Christian book. Barth's view stands against Bultmann's veiled Marcionite view that the Old Testament is the history of existential human failure. There is no Christ in Bultmann's Old Testament.

Barth's view stands against all Old Testament scholars who stand with the Jewish scholars and deny any Christological content in the Old Testament. It stands against the Old Testament scholars who see the unity of the Old and New Testaments in some non-Christological sense. And Barth's view stands against dispensationalism, which considers the harmony in Scripture to be found in the historical unfolding of seven dispensations.

The situation could only be met head on. The only real "universe of discourse" to understand Jesus Christ is the Old Testament. Christ cannot be abstracted from his history and culture and made into some kind of universal guru teaching proper things about prayer, religion, and morality. He is a messianic character from the Old Testament. Historic Christianity stands or falls with Jesus Christ understood in the context of the Old Testament. One cannot write any significant Christology that cuts Jesus off from the Old Testament. Therefore if Barth chose to keep the historic faith of the church, he had to once more reaffirm the Christological character of the Old Testament.

The Christological principle is procedural; it is an operational principle. It is a way of using the Old Testament for Christian teaching, proclamation, and interpretation. It is not an effort to achieve a systematic unity of Scripture by forcing all texts and passages into a system.

The Christological principle saves Holy Scripture for modern people. The people of the Enlightenment asked a very important question: "Why should we moderns be guided in our religion, our philosophy, and our morality by people of an ancient period of human history?" The conflict appeared in its most intense form under such captions as "The Quarrel of the Ancients and the Moderns" and "The Battle of the Books."[1]

Why should modern humanity be guided by the Mosiac laws of 3000 years ago? Or, why should we moderns be guided by Paul, a man of the Roman Empire? All these people lived and wrote before Galileo, Freud, and Einstein—before all the modern sciences.

The traditional answer has been that all these prophets and apostles, from Moses to Paul, wrote the Word of God under divine inspiration. Therefore they wrote timeless truth for all generations. God's Word is true in and for every generation.

One of Barth's most fundamental convictions is that the content of Christianity, not a formal theory of revelation or inspiration, makes Christianity believable. As far as doctrine of revelation and inspiration is concerned, there is none more purely formal than the Islamic view of the Koran. The earthly Koran is a perfect copy of a Koran in heaven with Allah. Even the most extreme view among Protestants of the inspiration of Scripture comes short of that. If the criteria for accepting a book as given of God are the highest and purest claims of divine revelation and inspiration, then we should all become Muslims.

Barth is therefore right in affirming that a person believes the Christian faith for the nature of its contents, not for its formal claims to revelation and inspiration. The Christology of Holy Scripture is the supreme content of the Christian faith. If one may use the word *apologetics* in this context, one could say that the only apologetics for Holy Scripture for modern people is the Christological content of Holy Scripture. And this content certainly means a Christology that includes the incarnation, the vicarious death, the bodily resurrection and ascension, and the return of Christ.

The Creed of Nicea is instructive at this point. It is a Christological-trinitarian confession in organization and content and affirms the central items of the Christian faith. In other words, it sells the Christian faith on the basis of that faith's content.

If modern persons take Holy Scripture seriously, they will do so for the Christological content of Scripture. The Christian faith cannot be established solely on a high view for revelation and inspiration. The best apologetic for the Scriptures is their Christological content.

------◦∞◦------

In the past few decades, a great deal of biblical study has been concerned with the study of Scripture from the perspective of the science of anthropology. The science of anthropology has discovered that every people has a culture—a set of complex patterns, rituals, and so on, whereby the people carries on its existence. This discovery means that the revelation that came through Israel, and then through Christ, and then to the apostles could come only dressed in garments of the prevailing culture. Therefore the clash between revelation and culture has become a sharp one. This clash has been especially central in deciding whether biblical statements about homosexuality and the status of women are culturally bound and therefore not applicable today, or whether they are revelational, applying to God's people for all time.

Another pressure on the biblical interpreter from the science of anthropology is the current discussion of culturally formed theology. Christians in Asia, Africa, and South America are protesting the dominance of a theology formed from the Greek-European tradition.

Barth's Christological approach to Scripture does not solve all the problems, but at least it provides a point of departure, a place of leverage, a means of handling problems. It may be stated this way: *the Christological principle gives us the center of the transcultural in Scripture.* The more a text or a passage or an ethical injunction can be tied in with Christology, the more likely we are dealing with the transcultural.

Barth knows that Christology itself is bound up with Jewish culture and says that we should not be ashamed or scandalized by the Jewish character of Scripture. The ancient Jewish people were elected by the grace of God to be the bearers of divine revelation. Therefore, our point of departure must be Israel and her culture. If we attempt to have a Christ totally abstracted from Jewish culture, we shall have a meaningless, formless Christ. Therefore, writing an Asian or African Christology can only be done by going from the Jesus and the culture of Israel to another Christology of another culture. One cannot abstract Christological ideas from the New Testament devoid of the culture of Israel and clothe them with garments of other cultures.

With that warning in mind, the positive gain of Barth's position can be exploited. Given a Scripture that reflects many cultures, and a church that exists in many cultures, the Christological principle gives us a point of stability so that all is not washed away by cultural relativism. And furthermore, as the church in many cultures works through its interpretation, theology, and ethics, it now at least has a canon to keep it on the right biblical and Christological track.

———⟨∞⟩———

All these issues are important for evangelicals. The unity of the Scripture is a problem with which every evangelical scholar of the Old or New Testament must come to terms. The Christological interpretation of the Old Testament is integral to evangelical theology. One of the most important tasks of evangelical theology is the correlation of its doctrine on the inspiration of Scripture with the content of Scripture (that is, the union of a formal with a material principle).

Barth does offer a paradigm for these matters. His solutions are not always the traditional ones, but they are alway very relevant to the issue. They show any evangelical scholar the contours of the problems, even if the solution may not be acceptable.

Note

1. See Gilbert Highet, *The Classical Tradition* (New York: Oxford University Press, 1957), chap. 14.

11

Freedom

FREEDOM WAS ONE of the great words of the Enlightenment. One of the oddities of language is that English has two words, *freedom* and *liberty*, but the German language only has one word (*Freiheit*), as does the French (*liberté*). Liberty (or freedom) was one of the key words of both the French and American revolutions, both of which occurred in the century of the Enlightenment.

The freedom of the Enlightenment was a positive concept. Granted, there must be freedom *from* oppression, tyranny, wicked forces, and all-powerful states. But the Enlightenment concept of freedom centered more on freedom *for*, freedom to *become*, freedom for *truth*, freedom to *develop*, and freedom to *explore*. Where human freedom is constrained, the human spirit is limited and dwarfed.

Unfortunately, the world still knows too much of oppressive states, military dictatorships, political prisoners, and brutal tortures. The Enlightenment's victory on the score of freedom was limited in both time and place. But for the true children of the Enlightenment, freedom is still one of the most precious things a person and a society can enjoy. Only in freedom can there be great science, great art, great literature, great education, and great human spirits.

It is among the children of the Enlightenment that Barth
must discuss his notion of freedom. And we find this amazing
paradox in Barth: he thinks as much of the worth of freedom
as does the most enthusiastic child of the Enlightenment, yet
he gives freedom a powerful Christian interpretation—which
in turn offends the children of the Enlightenment. Of course
Barth must defend the concept of freedom. The contemporary
children of the Enlightenment will have their freedom or they
won't have anything. Therefore Barth must have a powerful
theology of freedom if he wishes to reach the children of the
Enlightenment. And that he does. He almost parallels Schleiermacher in saying to the cultured despisers of religion that they
need not be offended by orthodoxy if they could only see it the
right way!

Barth has major discussions of freedom in the *Church Dogmatics* in two volumes (II/2, III/4)[1] and in a small pamphlet,
"Das Geschenk der Freiheit" ("The Gift of Freedom").

In the history of theology, the concept of the sovereignty of
God has some bad connotations. It suggests a theological determinism or an arbitrariness inconsistent with the nature of
God. It is a reminder of the dark side of Augustine's thought
and the hard side of Calvin's theology. If modern people want
anything, they want an open universe, even in their religion.
In liberal Christianity, tolerance is a great virtue and dogma-
tism a great vice, for tolerance is the voice of freedom. The
concept of the sovereignty of God also harks back to the God
of absolute arbitrary power worshiped by some medieval theologians. One could not love such a God. Perhaps it is this kind
of God that Sartre claimed would so crowd him that he would
cease to be a person and therefore on principle must be an
atheist.

To avoid all these bad connotations and yet retain that
which is essential in the concept of the sovereignty of God,
Barth must suggest another concept. This he does with his concept of the freedom of God.

With this concept, Barth wishes to correct the traditional concept of the sovereignty of God, but he also has a corrective aimed in another direction. The theologians of liberal Christianity had limited the freedom of God. They had said God is not free to become incarnate! God is not free to perform wonders! God is not free to reveal himself in a clear manner! God is not free to show wrath! God is not free to raise Christ from the dead! All these errors Barth wants to correct with his doctrine of the freedom of God.

------————<∞>————------

By freedom, Barth does not mean something like the logician's principle of indifference. A coin may come up—indifferently—heads or tails. A woman on occasion may buy a blue dress or a green one. Or a man may buy a pair of black shoes or brown ones. Nor does Barth mean the freedom to dress ourselves or to choose from a menu in a restaurant. He means the freedom that expresses our total selfhood, the freedom wherewith we conduct our lives in their totality, the freedom that expresses genuinely what we are, the freedom to become what we think we ought to be.

Applied to God, it means that God's freedom is not basically God's freedom to do anything, the freedom of unlimited possibility. It does not mean the freedom of formal majesty, as if God were the absolute, independent King of the universe. It does not mean the absolute power of disposal nor the freedom of naked sovereignty.

The freedom of God has a texture. The freedom of God is within a context of relationships. This concept is perfectly illustrated by the doctrine of the Trinity. The Father, Son, and Holy Spirit exist within the freedom of their mutual relationships. The freedom of God has the texture of encounter, fellowship, order, superordering, underordering, exaltation, humility, complete authority along with complete obedience, and the mutuality of gift and task.

In my opinion, one of the most unusual passages in the entire *Church Dogmatics* is one in which Barth eloquently describes the full range of the freedom of God. It pleads for full citation:

> It is not, then, the rigid presence of a being whose nature we can, so to speak, formulate in this or that principle. God is free to be present with the creature by giving Himself and revealing Himself to it or by concealing Himself and withdrawing Himself from it. God is free to be and operate in the created world either as unconditioned or as conditioned. God is free to perform His work either within the framework of what we call the laws of nature or outside it in the shape of miracle. God is free either to grant His immanence to nature by working at its heart or by exerting His sway at an infinite height above it. God is free to conceal His divinity from the creature, even to become a creature Himself, and free to assume again His Godhead. He is free to maintain as God His distance from the creature and equally free to enter into partnership with it, indeed, to lift the creature itself, in the most vigorous sense, into unity with His own divine being, with Himself. God is free to rule over the world in supreme majesty and likewise to serve in the world as the humblest and meanest of servants, free even to be despised in the world, and rejected by the world. God is free to clothe Himself with the life of the world in all its glory as with a garment; but free likewise Himself to die the death which symbolises the end of all things earthly, in utter abandonment and darkness. God is free to be entirely unlimited over against the world: not bound by its finitude, nor by its infinitude; not confined to its time and space as a whole, nor to any one area of space or period of time. He is equally free to limit Himself: to be eternal in the tiny endlessness of our starry heavens, or of our human conceptuality, but eternal also in our finitude; to be shut up in the totality of our time-space universe, but also in all humility to be confined to this or that time and place as contrasted with other times and places. God is free to ally Himself, within creation, to the spirit as against rebellious nature, but also free to ally Himself with nature in opposition to the undoubtedly more rebellious spirit. God is free to be provoked and to be merciful, to bless and to punish, to kill and to make alive, to exalt us to heaven and to cast us down into hell. God is free to be wholly inward to the creature and at the same time

as Himself wholly outward: *totus intra et totus extra* and both, of course, as forms of His immanence, of His presence, of the relationship and communion chosen, willed and created by Himself between Himself and His creation. This is how He meets us in Jesus Christ. His revelation in Jesus Christ embraces all these apparently so diverse and contradictory possibilities. They are all His possibilities. If we deny Him any one of them, we are denying Jesus Christ and God Himself. Instead of recognising and adoring God, we are setting up an idol. For we are imposing upon Him—in defiance of the freedom which He has actually proved to us—a bondage which can be only that of our own self-will that would like to deny God and put itself in the place of God. If only the Word of God breaks through the walls of our self-will, our worship of the freedom of God exercised in His immanence can have no bounds. And then the full inadequacy of all pantheism and panentheism will be exposed to us. For what a poor limited God it is, and what a poor and limited world, whose confines wholly or partially overlap in these systems, so that they have to be wholly or partially interpreted as a unity! Once the boundless exaltation of God's freedom in immanence is recognised to be necessary and rendered, there can be no further lapse into these systems.[2]

Having established the freedom of God, Barth establishes the freedom of man—but in a most unusual manner. In harmony with the Enlightenment, he grants man its full freedom. But as the Christian critic of the Enlightenment, he establishes human freedom on the most vigorous Christian theological grounds.

Human freedom is a gift, a present from God (*Geschenk*). God's freedom is prior to human freedom. The free God has freely chosen to be our God, Lord, Shepherd. In God's free choice to be our God, he also gives us freedom. In turn, we are to joyfully and thankfully recognize this freedom from God and to ratify in our own lives both the choice and the gift of God. In this relationship, we are God's creatures, God's covenant partners, and God's children. True human freedom is living life on Earth in this relationship.

This definition of freedom has a number of subtheses. First of all, there is no neutral concept of freedom, no abstract philosophical definition of freedom, no typical Arminian concept of man as "free moral agent." Human freedom is a pure gift of grace issuing from God's freedom.

I have mentioned that God's freedom has both texture and a set of relationships. The same is true with man. We understand the richness of our freedom only in revelation, which means only in Scripture. Therefore, we learn the first great lesson of our freedom from the Gospel of Jesus Christ. And in turn the Gospel is set in the larger context of salvation history (Barth uses the word *Heilsgeschichte*).

One of the central theses that Barth develops is that the two concepts of freedom (of God and of man) perfectly mesh. If the relationship is a proper one, then God in his freedom and man in his freedom coexist in a happy, joyful manner. Sin is then defined as the abuse of this freedom, which leads to slavery. The sinner is not a free person but a slave. The only truly free person is the Christian, using his or her gift of freedom to live before God.

Barth summarized his views of God's freedom and human freedom in a lecture he gave, *"Das Geschenk der Freiheit"* ("The Gift of Freedom"), which was to correlate the concept of freedom with Christian ethics. But he concluded the lecture with an unusual twist. To illustrate his concept of freedom, he set out the criteria for a free theologian, which further serves as a window on Barth's concept of freedom. Barth lists five items to illustrate the freedom of the theologian, summarized here:

1. The point of beginning for the free theologian is the resurrection of Jesus Christ. This context sets the theologian in the proper stance. The resurrection determines the nature of his or her willingness, readiness, and capability to be a theologian. This priority of the resurrection of Christ gives the free theologian a window toward heaven, the skylight (*Oberlicht*) without which he or she could not be a free, happy theologian. This position also means that

theology is fundamentally an act of prayer, a giving of thanks and of requests, a liturgical action.

2. The free theologian comes softly and happily to the Bible. He or she does not come to defend any kind of orthodoxy but to hear the Word of God. The analytical approach to Scripture has its place (the historical-critical method, the fund of information we have about Scripture), but the analytical method has its limitations. There must also be the synthetic method. In the synthetic method of the study of Scripture, the interpreter's primary task is to hear the Word of God in the text. And this task calls prayer and meditation into play. From what the interpreter has heard in Scripture, he or she now must formulate as well as possible a systematic theology but must always retain the freedom to hear the Word of God in the Scripture. In other words, the free theologian whose first priority is the defense of orthodoxy will lose his or her freedom; as will one who studies the Scriptures only analytically.

3. The free theologian knows, confesses, and admits that he or she cannot write theology without using some philosophy. It belongs to human creatureliness to use philosophy. The question is "How is philosophy used?" The theologian who capitulates to any philosophy loses his or her freedom. But the theologian who knows what to do with philosophy may use philosophy and not lose freedom.

4. The free theologian works in the church. There is the great tradition of fathers in the church, such as Luther and Calvin, who admitted there were fathers before them. And there are also very important people in church administration, such as bishops. The theologian ought not be resentful of the administration of the church (*ein antikirchenregimentliches Ressentiment!*). The theologian who recognizes fathers in the church, the necessity of church officials, and of church administration will not be a sectarian. A sectarian theologian under-

stands freedom as freedom *from*. The free theologian understands his freedom as freedom *for*. The sectarian theologian is a private theologian. But private theology is not theology and is therefore not free!

5. The free theologian works in communication with other theologians. Granted, it is not always a peaceful task. Theologians can write bitter things about each other. Barth says that one can find these items of bitterness in book reviews and footnotes. The free theologian is always a positive theologian, always a theologian in fellowship. To be otherwise is to lose one's freedom.

————·◦∞◦·————

How, then, is Barth a paradigm for evangelical theology and its concept of freedom? What has Barth gained in his theology of freedom?

First, he certainly has come to terms with the concept of freedom as it has flowed out of the Enlightenment until today. It is not difficult to discover that one of the most fundamental objections to the Christian faith is that to become a Christian costs a person his or her freedom. Any teacher of theology who has often reviewed the theology of Augustine and Calvin knows the quiet rebellion of students against a theology that smells like determinism. The modern world will only hear of a theology of freedom. The first virtue of Barth is to meet that concept head on.

Having met it head on, he does not capitulate to the Enlightenment understanding of freedom. Instead, he gives the concept a profound theological reinterpretation. He grounds human freedom in the freedom of God. He says that the usual definition of freedom that people write for themselves is a definition of sin. He grounds freedom in the trinity, in divine revelation, in salvation history, and in the Gospel.

Second, another advantage of Barth's definition of freedom is that it preserves the spirituality and dignity of human freedom. Standing in freedom as a gift of God, we are totally free. Because freedom is a gift, it can be abused. It is not a forced gift. The price of abusing it is not more freedom and fewer restraints, but slavery—the loss of freedom.

Barth's "third way" in this debate is to avoid the determinism that shadows the Calvinist version and the notorious "freedom of the will" of Arminian theology (for Barth believes that the root of religious liberalism was Arminianism). Instead, he postulates the mutual interfacing of divine freedom with human freedom, the latter a gift of grace of the former.

Fourth, in the older debates between orthodox theologians and theologians of liberal Christianity, the orthodox argued for the strong authority of Scripture and for the need to subject all human thought to the Word of God. However, this requirement also carried an overtone of threat to human freedom. Barth has turned things around in his doctrine of freedom, so that the only truly free people are Christians. And thereby he has given a paradigm in how to argue for orthodox, historic Christianity without threatening the concept of freedom.

Notes

1. Barth, *CD*, II/2 and III/4.
2. Barth, *CD*, II/1, pp. 314–315.

12

Ethics

THE GREATEST ETHICAL TREATISE of the Enlightenment was Kant's *Critique of Practical [Moral] Reason*. Its purpose was to show that the basic rule of ethics could be deduced from Reason (*Vernunft*). Kant wrote three great critiques centering on Reason: *The Critique of Pure Reason*, or science; *The Critique of Practical Reason*, or morality; and *The Critique of Judgment*, or beauty.

The traditional Christian stance had been that ethics depends on religion or theology. In other words, ethics is not a self-contained discipline; its validity depends on something outside it. Both the ethical rules and the sanctions (of blessing and judgment) derive from religion. In a magisterial way, Kant attempted to prove that ethics is a self-contained discipline. The philosopher can deduce the ethical rule from Reason, and from Reason alone. In simplest terms, Reason tells us that a given ethical action is right if it can be universalized. Stealing cannot be universalized, for universal stealing would destroy the fabric of society. Love can be universalized, because love works for the good of all people.

If Kant is right, then Reason can supply us with our system of ethics. Ethics has been made autonomous. It has been cut off

144

from religion and theology. Even though Kant believed in God, freedom, and immortality, these too were deliveries of Reason.

A self-contained ethical system means that an ethical rule is followed because it is good in itself. It is intrinsically good. If a person does good because religion or God tells him or her what the good is, then the good is not intrinsically good, because it depends on something else for its validity. The mature person of the Enlightenment follows Kant's advice: "Dare to think!" Stand on your own feet! Be mature! The good is good intrinsically! Nobody should ever dare to do a proposed act if its ethical support were not intrinsically good. Ethics does not depend on divine revelation.

To do the good for any other reason is to be immature, childish, dependent. We have our Reason, which guides us to the norm of all ethics, to the intrinsic good, to the mature way of behaving. Ethics so understood is independent of divine revelation or religion. It is an autonomous discipline.

This has been the story of ethics in philosophical studies since Kant. Kant is not the only source of modern ethical theory, but he towers in the landscape. Other ethical theories such as utilitarianism and its pragmatic rule of the most good for the most number of people, have cut ethics off from religion. Some have also defended the proposition that the good is an indefinable yet real thing, like the color yellow. In any case, the result is the same. For one reason or another, ethics is cut off from religion or from divine revelation and has become a self-contained discipline. The good is the instrinsically good, or the utilitarian good, or the intuited good.

Barth has written extensively on ethics. The second half of *Church Dogmatics* II/2 contains his basic ethical theory, and the entire volume of *Church Dogmatics* III/4 is devoted to particular ethical topics.

Barth's discussion of ethics is predominantly continental and German, although he makes some reference to French writers. He is aware of the British utilitarians Jeremy Bentham and John Mill, but mentions them only in passing. He does not seem aware of the great British contributions to the subject from the earlier twentieth-century Oxford specialists in ethics, to the later writers in the linguistic school. However, Kant has been a lifelong concern of Barth's so he has mastered the theory of the master. Much of the later linguistic or analytic school of philosophy can be found in essence in Kant, so in knowing Kant Barth at least knows the heart of the linguistic school.

Barth's problem in ethical theory is to restate in a meaningful way the historic Christian stance toward ethics and theology for a readership that has been for the most part convinced by the Enlightenment that ethics is to be cut off from religion and revelation. He faces other problems, too! In Nazi and Marxist theory, the good is determined by the state. In Roman Catholic and liberal Christianity, the good is defined in a preliminary step by philosophy. In existential philosophy, the good is the product of our own creation or projection.

There is still another major problem. In theological education, ethics has become a separate discipline. In some larger theological schools, it has become a department. Even in Basel, where Barth was professor of theology, Hendrik van Oyen was professor of ethics. Furthermore, philosophical ethics has spilled over from the university into theological education as theological ethics. And the materials in ethics and its subdivisions have become so large only a specialist can manage them. Still further, the Kantian redefinition of religion as primarily ethics has pushed seminary education more in the direction of ethics. Barth wants to end this division of ethics and theology, for very profound theological reasons.

Barth does not return ethics to theology on the basis of the doctrine of the Middle Ages known as the absolute power of God (*potesta absoluta*). It was argued that the moral rule was arbitrarily decreed by a sovereign God. God could reverse the Ten Commandments if he so willed. The only rule he need keep is that of consistency among the rules he announces. This kind of theological thinking is based on the most abstract concept of God and is therefore totally different from the God of Holy Scripture.

Barth returns ethics to the territory of theology by including ethics in the fundamental doctrine of God. Barth is famous for the manner in which he relocates topics in his own ordering of his *Church Dogmatics*. It has been customary to discuss ethics under the doctrine of sanctification. Ethics in the form of the Christian life forms a large part of Book 3 of Calvin's *Institutes of the Christian Religion*. Barth's second volume (*Band* 2) is devoted to the doctrine of God, and it is in that volume that he introduces his basic ethical theory.

If Barth had discussed God in one place of the *Church Dogmatics* and ethics in another place, then he would already have lost the game. He would have acknowledged the rightness of splitting ethics away from theology. But that split would separate the idea of God from the idea of the good—the very maneuver philosophical ethics seeks to accomplish. Barth's position is that one must think of both the idea of God and the idea of the good at the same time. To put it simply, whoever has said *God* has already said *good*; or, whoever says *theology* has already said *ethics*. To think of God without a command of God (that is, an ethical imperative) is to think a contradictory thought. There is no interval between pronouncing the name of God and the command of God. The God of Holy Scripture cannot be thought of for one millionth of a second as separate from his holiness, and when one thinks of a holy God one has already thought of ethics.

Those who want to make the good intrinsically good, and hence independent from God, turn ethics loose in the world like an orphan. Ethics is thus expected to live and survive on its own autonomous strength. Such a view of the separation of ethics and religion certainly pleases the philosophers, for they can give their lectures and write their books in happy isolation from troublesome religion. But such an orphan can hardly survive in any healthy way in the evil, wicked, depraved world, whose depravity is heavily documented by every daily edition of the newspaper. Fyodor Dostoyevsky wrote in *The Brothers Karamazov* that if there is no God nor immortality nor natural law, then it is entirely possible that all our vices could be converted into virtues. Even cannibalism could become a virtue. Such is the fate of morality if ethics is made an orphan. In the modern mood of the most extreme permissiveness in our society Dostoyevsky's words are coming to pass.

By putting ethics into the doctrine of God, Barth has certainly ended the notion that ethical rules are arbitrary. Moral rules are not the impositions of a God whose sovereignty is abstract and infinite. He has also put an end to the notion that the idea of God and the idea of the intrinsic good are incompatible. This divorce is shown graphically in Jean-Paul Sartre's little book *Existentialism*, in which he discusses the process of decision making. Sartre presents a young Frenchman in the agony of an ethical decision. In reviewing critically the options open to the young man and the kind of resolution Sartre comes to, it is apparent that Sartre clearly separates the idea of God from the good. According to Barth, God has a distinct "personality." He is not an abstract God. In God's person is deeply imbedded the good, the loving, the gracious, and the holy. *If God is intrinsically good*—that is where the rub is!—then God's command is intrinsically good and morality and religion have been reunited.

This argument can be put another way. The God of Holy Scripture is simultaneously creator, redeemer, and moral lord. To confess one name is to immediately confess the others. A philosopher would violate the biblical revelation if he or she first proved that God is and *then* attempted to prove that such a God is also holy.

Barth's discussion of ethics provides extensive materials on the nature of the good. This provision is important, because a high-level discussion of the good has been sustained in British publications on ethics (e.g., those by W. D. Ross, G. E. Moore). From a number of different sets of arguments, the conclusions drawn are usually that (1) ethics can (and ought to, according to Bertrand Russell) be separated from religion; and (2) the good is intrinsically good. The notion that the good is intrinsic is stated by Kant, even though not as starkly as by the British philosophers. Barth over and over again affirms that the concept of the good and the concept of God are intimately joined. A good God commands only the good. Whether Barth has succeeded or not is debatable; that he has put his finger at the most critical point of ethical theory cannot be debated. Barth has made the best case he can to rejoin the Christian doctrine of God and the concept of the good.

However, the attempt to bond together God and the good is only part of Barth's basic ethical theory. Barth aims at writing an ethics that is at the same time biblical, Christological, and redemptive. Barth wrote two beautiful paragraphs in reference to this.[1] In the first, he describes the God of Christian ethics. He is the God and Father of our Lord Jesus Christ. In the second, he describes humanity as the object of Christian ethics. The human being is the person created and loved by God. This position stands in marked and wonderful contrast to philosophical and even theological works on ethics that give barren if not ascetic descriptions of God as "moral author" and the human being as "moral subject."

In rugged consistency with his Christological principle, Barth limits his ethical theory to the revelation of God attested to in Holy Scripture. Therefore he rejects philosophical ethics. He thinks that both Roman Catholicism and religious liberalism find a beginning of Christian ethics in philosophical ethics. They are both guilty of the same error. Anybody who attempts to create an ethics of natural law also comes under Barth's judgment. He views the relationship of biblical ethics to that of philosophical ethics as that of Joshua and his army taking over the Promised Land. Acre by acre, Christian ethics must gradually displace philosophical ethics.

Barth's ethics can help evangelical ethics in the following ways. First, he is certainly right in bringing ethics back under the umbrella of theology. Evangelical schools have gone the way of schools of liberal Christianity in setting up a chair or department of ethics separate from the department of theology. This trend is especially unfortunate because the professor of ethics may have no more than an amateur's education in theology. People like Helmut Thielicke, Karl Barth, and Dietrich Bonhoeffer show (in my opinion) the necessity of a thorough grounding in theology prior to specialization in ethics.

Second, Barth is certainly right in challenging the notion that the perception of good as intrinsically good justifies the separation of theology and ethics. As far as philosophers as a class of scholars are concerned, the definition of the good as intrinsic has happily led to the separation of religion and ethics. Now ethics can be discussed without dragging God into the discussion. However, on Barth's side is the structure of the Ten Commandments: the first four are theology and are the presuppositions on which are based the last six, which are the more conventional ethical imperatives.

Third, Barth's anchoring of ethics in Christology has yet another important advantage. When the Christian church talks about moral issues in society apart from Jesus Christ, it impresses the populace as being prudish, moralistic, and isolated from the passions of the marketplace. Barth set a model for evangelicals in his pastorate. He would not speak to the labor or union groups without mentioning Jesus Christ, and he would not preach Jesus Christ in his church without commenting on social issues. By keeping ethics and Christology so close, Barth goes a long way toward preventing the church, in its ethical witness, as appearing only moralistic, only prudish, only interested in principles and not people.

Note

1. Barth, *CD*, III/4, pp. 24–25.

13

The Doctrine of Man

THE ENLIGHTENMENT confused the doctrine of man and developments since then have been even more confusing. Philip Rhinelander's book is entitled *Is Man Incomprehensible to Man?* and the answer is apparently yes. There is no common agreement among scientists, psychologists, psychiatrists, sociologists, philosophers, or theologians about that common element that forms humanity. Since the Enlightenment, we have had a multitude of approaches to human beings: Freudian psychoanalytic, Marxist economic, Comtian sociological, Watsonian behavioral, Wilsonian sociobiological, existentialist self-creating.

National and international life depends on a common definition of humanity. Educational theory, psychiatric theory, criminal justice theory, and so on all depend on some basic theory of the nature of the human person.

In many places in *Church Dogmatics*, Barth reveals that he recognizes this difficult modern problem of defining the nature of man (Mensch). He is most keenly aware of the extensive efforts of Heidegger, Jaspers, and Sartre to redefine man in the twentieth century. Accordingly, in the *Church Dogmatics*

Barth has attempted to give his theological definition of humanity.

Barth's doctrine of man is set in the largest context of cosmology. In speaking of cosmology in the Christian context, the Christian scholar is faced with the problem of the relationship between the first chapters of Genesis (and the cosmological picture presupposed there) and the kind of cosmos depicted by modern science.

The problem can be sharply put this way. (1) On the one hand, revelation does not set out the details of the manner in which the cosmos is put together in anticipation of modern science. Yet (2) if the Old Testament is a prescientific book, how can it escape the errors of a prescientific cosmology?

One way of handling this problem is to make a distinction between a world view (*Weltanschauung*) and a world picture (*Weltbild*). One's theological and/or philosophical view of reality is one's world view; one's understanding of how the cosmos is put together is one's world picture. Hence the world view of Genesis is binding revelation, but the world picture is not. This distinction has been defended by Eric C. Rust in his book *Science and Faith*.

Another way of resolving the problem of a revelation written in a prescientific period and yet retaining current authority is to make a distinction between the literary genre of the passage and its theological message. The genre is prescientific, the message is theological. Roman Catholic scholars are permitted to classify the genre as Oriental (i.e. Middle-Eastern) and symbolic, even poetic. James Orr, the great Reformed theologian, followed a similar strategy in his effort to harmonize the biblical record with modern scientific knowledge. The Oriental genre is the vehicle through which the revelation comes and is not binding; but the theological message it conveys *is* binding.

------·◇·------

In *Church Dogmatics* (II/2), Barth faces the issue of Genesis and science in a manner rare in his writings. In his comments, Barth reveals that he knows very well the outlines of modern science. Although he had little passion for science as such, he was not as unlettered in science as some thought him. It should also be mentioned that teaching in a small, compact university structure, in contrast to our sprawling American universities, Barth had intimate contact with university scientists as well as having many friends who were scientists in different fields (including psychiatry).

His first step is to let the Genesis record stand as it is, a product of the prescientific world with its prescientific cosmologies. Without question, the cosmological backdrop in Genesis 2 is different from the backdrop in Genesis 1. Furthermore, between Genesis 1 and Revelation 22 many other cosmologies are introduced. According to Barth, the only sensible thing is to admit the multiplicity. In this connection, Barth makes one of his rare comments on obscurantism. He says it has never won a battle—so why fight over the many biblical cosmologies?

Barth's second step is to tell us that this multiplicity should not distress us. Christian theologians have used all kinds of cosmologies, from Plato's famous *Timaeus* to Aristotle's, Ptolemy's, Newton's, and Einstein's. Yet the diversity has not disturbed our theological craftsmanship. There is no common cosmology behind Sacred Scripture. There is no common cosmology behind Christian theology. So therefore the cosmological issue should not be a big issue in the Scriptures nor Christian theology. If one demands that the Scripture be innocent in the matter of cosmology, then we could not write theology until Einstein!

The third step is to assert that these texts (Genesis 1–3) are the Word of God. The Word of God is "in, with, and under" the cosmology. The cosmology is not the Word of God, but the message within the cosmology is the Word of God. Revelation does not intend to teach science, and therefore the Word of God is independent of the cosmology. Therefore neither Holy Scripture or Christian theology is involved in teaching cosmology. The theological teaching of the text does not compete with modern cosmological explanations of the universe. There is neither conflict nor harmony, for they are explanations of different orders.

The fourth step is to outline the precise nature of the work of scientists and of theologians.[1]

1. If scientists do their work in theory construction within the limits of the data themselves, scientists will never say anything contrary to the Word of God. If scientists convert their theories into world views, then it could well be that such world views could conflict with the Word of God. For example, if physicists were to convert physics into the metaphysics of materialism, they would conflict with the Word of God.

2. If theologians restrict themselves to the Word of God and pure theological statements about humanity, heaven, and earth, then theologians will never say anything contrary to science. But if theologians propose to also teach science in the name of theology, they then may well run counter to current scientific knowledge.

Both scientists and theologians are to be governed in their methodology strictly by the nature of the subject investigated. Science and theology are both to be completely determined by the nature of the subject matter they investigate. Or, they are to be severely restricted to their very special subject matters. Taking such care in metholodology removes the conflict between science and theology, between theologian and scientist. Those familiar with the writings of C. S. Lewis will note how similarly Barth and Lewis thought, although they wrote in drastically different styles and contexts (see "The Funeral of a Great Myth" [Evolution], in *Christian Reflections*).

------◇------

Having set up his belief about cosmology in Scripture and theology, and the relationship of science and theology, Barth then turns to the doctrine of man. Barth reviews all sorts of efforts to show empirically that the human being is superior to animals. Some have tried to prove it by comparing the human brain with the animal brain. Others have appealed to human ethical powers; others, to human rational powers; and others, to human existential nature to show how human beings transcend the animal. All make a point, but none make a case. They can show that the human being is different from animals, but they cannot show how he or she uniquely transcends the animals so as to be a creature of a different order. They prove the human being as "superanimal" but not as "superhuman" (human in the image of God).

The essence of Barth's doctrine of man (Mensch) is based on his distinction between phenomenal man and real man. Phenomenal man is all that we know of man from all our human sciences. Real man is man as he is known in divine revelation. We cannot derive real man from phenomenal man and that is the error in all efforts to find the real man by comparative anatomy or comparative psychology.

The Word of God tells us about the real man. The real man is man as he is before God. Neither science nor psychology nor philosophy nor general religious knowledge can reveal the real man. Barth is even more precise. The nature of the real man is revealed in the human nature of Jesus Christ. Hence Barth's doctrine is not only a revealed doctrine of man but a Christological doctrine of man.

In that the phenomenal man and the real man are known by two totally separate methods, our knowledge of the two does not conflict. The psychiatrist and sociologist are not competing with the theologian, so the theologian need not deny any knowledge of humanity they offer. Nor can studies in the phenomenal man challenge that which we know of the real man in the Word of God.

Barth suggests here and there that maybe in the future connections will be found between science and revelation. Such a discovery would also mean connections between our knowledge of phenomenal man and of real man. Barth does not intend a radical disjunction between the two ways of knowing man. But at the present time, in the current state of theology, he has felt impelled to make such sharp disjunctions. Too much theology is based on studies of phenomenal man; for example, in existential theology. Therefore the radical distinction between phenomenal man and real man must be drawn before we can think of how they can be correlated.

------◦◦◦------

The doctrine of man also involves a theology of Heaven and Earth. Heaven is the sphere of God; Earth is the sphere of man. These are not cosmological conceptions; rather, they are theological and relational concepts. Biblical anthropology is about man on Earth in relationship to God in his Heaven. There is then no conflict or contest between the notions of Heaven and Earth with relationship to our understanding of the scientific notions of the Earth and the rest of space.

My purpose is not to reproduce Barth's thought in detail but to give an idea of his methodology. I note in his doctrine of man no obscurantism, but likewise no concessionism. He does not challenge certain elements of biblical criticism nor modern scientific learning. He is not obscurantist about biblical criticism or science. On this score Barth does not bypass the Enlightenment and modern learning. But neither does he concede to the Enlightenment or biblical criticism or modern science in setting out the biblical and theological doctrine of man. The liberal theologians were wrong in making such concessions to modern learning and by so doing lost the integrity of Christian theology. Fundamentalists do not properly interact with modern learning and are thus condemned to the losing strategy of obscurantism.

------◦◦◦------

Evangelicals have had their problems with their doctrine of man. They have had to deny that there is an ancient cosmology in the Book of Genesis. They have had been perplexed with the apparent recency of man according to Genesis and the radically longer history of man as presented by the science of anthropology. Some evangelicals have handled the problems by denying outright all biblical criticism and the theory of evolution. Others have tried some sort of compromise between biblical criticism, anthropological science, and the biblical view of man. Still others have attempted to show on biological, physiological, or psychological grounds that human beings are so different from the highest primates that they must be in the image of God. In all this, there is some measure of obscurantism.

On the surface, Barth's solution has the best of both worlds. Under the concept of phenomenal man he can let the sciences claim all they wish about man and yet insist that they come short of the final assessment. Under the concept of real man he can claim all a Christian theologian needs to claim about man being in the image of God, yet not contradict any of the sciences. No doubt the theory has some weaknesses. This distinction between the phenomenal man and the real man may be too artificial. Perhaps we can learn so much of the phenomenal man we may ignore the real man. But the strengths in Barth's position can help evangelical theology. Barth does not have to engage in obscurantism either with reference to biblical criticism or the sciences. And he does give us a working solution so that we can have some means of correlating the vast knowledge of man attained by the sciences with what we believe is the most important dimensions of man gained by divine revelation.

Note

1. Barth, *CD*, II/2, pp. 12–13.

14

The Existence of God

PROOFS FOR THE EXISTENCE of God ("theistic proofs") have a long history. Some of the most distinguished philosophers— such as Plato, Aristotle, Augustine, Thomas, Anselm, Descartes, Berkeley, and Hegel—have defended one proof or another or a group of proofs. Thomas is famous for setting out five proofs for the existence of God; some have said, one proof in five versions. Anselm is famous for the ontological proof (so named by Kant), and Kant is famous for the moral proof for the existence of God.

The theistic proofs have been urged by theologians and apologists on the basis that such proofs create a moral and logical disposition for the truth of the Christian faith. If one can prove that God exists, one is halfway toward proving Christianity true. Accordingly, there has been a close relationship in the history of Christian theology between philosophical theism and Christian theology. Cardinal Newman argued in *The Idea of a University* that theology must be part of a university curriculum because it has had a long history from the Greeks onward as a major concern of education and philosophical thought and is not something provincial within the church. Furthermore, if a person can prove the existence of God on philosophical grounds, then he or she has shown that Christian faith is in harmony with sound philosophical reasoning.

But the Enlightenment challenged all this! David Hume, the Scottish philosopher, is the great critic of the traditional Christian apologetics. Most current skepticism in Academia and among philosophers has its origin in Hume's philosophical writings. His writings, in turn, stimulated the great Immanuel Kant and forced him to rethink his entire philosophical program. In rethinking his program (*The Critique of Pure Reason*), Kant came to two conclusions about the theistic proofs.

First, the very nature of our knowledge is such that we cannot make meaningful statements about God. An ingredient of every meaningful statement is some sense perception, and God is never a sense perception. Therefore, in principle, a priori, any theistic proof is excluded from valid human knowledge. A theistic proof is outside the bounds of scientific reason (*Vernunft*).

Second, Kant showed that the proofs for the existence of God were all specious in their argumentation. An argument is judged specious if it appears on first reading to be in good order but when critically analyzed its logic comes apart. He also argued that any theistic interpretation of man or the universe was as alien to pure reason as any theistic proof. Although Kant believed in God for moral reasons (*The Critique of Practical [Moral] Reason*), his attack on the traditional theistic proofs was devastating.

Some philosophers in the twentieth century have not given up on the proofs. From time to time, a fresh discussion breaks out in even the most distinguished of philosophical journals. But if one judges the general picture, Hume and Kant dealt a blow to traditional philosophical theism and Christian apologetics from which the Christian faith has never recovered, at least among the children of the Enlightenment. The greater number of scholars and professors—the learned people, the intelligentsia—believe that Hume and Kant ended the rational case for Christianity.

It is at this point where Barth must begin. Of all the philosophers, he perhaps knew Kant the most thoroughly, for Barth's university training in philosophy was among the neo-Kantians. His long essay on Kant in *Protestant Theology in the Nineteenth Century* reveals his great familiarity with Kant's thought. Although he only mentions Hume once in the *Church Dogmatics,* nobody can study Kant and not study Hume. So Barth knows well the demolition work done by these two philosophers. From time to time in the *Church Dogmatics* he refers at length to Jaspers, Heidegger, and Sartre, so he knows where the current argument is. He does not seem aware of the writings of the Vienna Circle of positivists and their American and British followers. But this is not too great a loss, for this movement admits that its original mentors are Hume and Kant.

Barth does not talk of the proof for the existence of God, but rather of the knowledge of God. This concept is treated extensively in *Church Dogmatics,* and, as usual with Barth, I cannot begin to treat the richness of those many pages.[1] I limit myself to some leading notions of Barth about the existence of God.

With Calvin, Barth takes a sturdy stand on this matter: *the knowledge of the existence of God is inseparably bound up with the saving experience of the Gospel of Jesus Christ and may not be meaningfully discussed apart from it.*

Hume and Kant were right for the wrong reasons! They were right in affirming that philosophical reasoning cannot bring a person to a true knowledge of God. The real reason why this is not possible is because a human being is a sinner. A sinner by definition is a rebel, an enemy, a spiritually blind person. Sinners can be reached by God only with a Gospel. Therefore, according to Scripture the knowledge that God exists *for sinners* must be bound up with the Gospel of Jesus Christ, which is *for sinners.* The Enlightenment is not so much to be fought (as it so sturdily is in much evangelical apologetics) as it is to be ignored!

Barth's attitude toward the existence of God comes out in his reference to a number of different theologians and biblical passages.

First, he responds to *Anselm*, the great theologian of the Middle Ages, who set forth the ontological argument for the existence of God, which presumed to prove that God exists solely from philosophical considerations. Barth revolutionized the study of Anselm by turning him around 180 degrees. Barth sees Anselm's argument as a lesson in clarification: having come to believe in God by grace, what order of being do we presume God to be? Only prayer, faith, salvation, and the Holy Spirit can convey to a person the reality of God! But once we have come to the knowledge of God that way, we may seek to understand in sharper lines the God in whom we believe.

Second, Barth never tires of attacking Thomas, his analogy of being, and the philosophical theism that Roman Catholic theology has built on that analogy. The arguments and counterarguments fly thick, both theologically and philosophically, so I only intend to state Barth's basic intention.

By natural theology, Barth means any effort to prove the existence of God apart from the saving knowledge of God in Jesus Christ. He sees the two chief defenders of natural theology as Roman Catholic theologians and religious liberal theologians. According to Barth, it is theologically and spiritually confusing, if not chaos, to affirm that there are two valid means of knowing God: one in natural theology and the other in revealed theology. The whole *raison d'être* of revealed theology is that a natural theology is impossible. Accordingly, Barth does not see natural theology as only a case of bad logic or poor theology. He sees it as the act of the sinner's spiritual rebellion. It is the sinner's stronghold against the true knowledge of God in the revelation of God in Jesus Christ.

Third, although Barth and Brunner have much in common in their theology of revelation and the Christological principle in theology, Brunner believed that there was a second task of theology (as he called it); namely, to prove that there was a general revelation but not a natural theology. This provoked from Barth his famous, wrathful *Nein! Antwort an Emil Brunner* ("No! Answer to Emil Brunner"). His point is that Brunner, no less than Roman Catholic philosophical theism, breaks up the biblical pattern of belief that we only know God through Jesus Christ.

Fourth, the customary interpretation of Romans 2 is that the Gentiles have a knowledge of God in their hearts separate from the knowledge that the Jews have in their law or Torah. Hence there are two knowledges of God, one for Jews, another for Gentiles. Of course, Barth's doctrine of the exclusive knowledge of God in Jesus Christ cannot coexist with the traditional interpretation.

Barth actually wrote three commentaries on Romans. The last was a very small book composed of popular lectures to high school teachers. It sums up the position he had come to about Romans in the writing of the *Church Dogmatics*. Barth's basic stance is that Romans 1:16–17 specifies the point of view from which Paul writes. That point is the revelation of the righteousness of God in the Gospel of Jesus Christ. Therefore, he never shifts to any neutral, philosophical, or sociological-descriptive point from Romans 1:18 to Romans 3:20. There is no separate, independent treatment of creation in Romans 1:18–20, nor of the Jew or the Gentile in Romans 2. All is surveyed from the perspective of Romans 1:16–17. Hence there is only one true knowledge of God, and that is in the Gospel of Jesus Christ. There is no second knowledge in creation, nor third in the Jewish Torah, nor fourth in the conscience of the Gentile.

Max Bense, a professor of philosophy at Stuttgart, published a brief essay in defense of atheism in a Zurich newspaper. Barth was asked to reply (in *Fragments Grave and Gay*). Although the reply is brief and popularly written, it expresses Barth's central conviction.

Barth replies to Bense that the knowledge of God and his existence that the Christians have is a pure gift of God's grace. God comes to us! We are literally invaded by God. How can a Christian defend this? If two scholars have different theories about some phenomenon or problem, a debate is in order. The

Christian knowledge of God is not the product of human thought, philosophy, or theology. It is something posited by God in revelation, grace, and salvation. Hence it cannot be debated, as can other controversial issues. It can be accepted in gratitude, faith, and obedience, or it can be rejected; but it cannot be debated.

Barth then proceeds to attack Bense with a notion found in a number of places in Barth's thought. Every person puts his or her world together in some manner. The manner in which each person puts his or her world of experience together is that person's theology and religion. Barth notes how passionately Bense argues for his atheism. Therefore it is not a case of Bense's atheism versus Barth's Christian theism; rather, it is a case of Bense's religious atheistic theism versus Barth's Christian theism.

———————

How, then, is Barth's approach to the existence of God a paradigm or help for evangelical theology?

It is obvious to me that we cannot return to the confidence in theistic proofs that existed before Hume and Kant. The attack on them launched by Hume and Kant has been kept alive by naturalists, materialists, realists, positivists, and those of the analytic or linguistic school. There have been efforts to revive one or more of them but that has been done in an intellectual atmosphere not congenial to their reception. The confession that they are morally persuasive even if not logically or "mathematically" persuasive means that, in the last analysis, they are specious arguments.

Some have tried to revive one or more of these arguments by correcting some of the logical faults in the earlier versions. In the earlier part of this century, F. R. Tennant attempted to reformulate the argument from design. Charles Hartshorne and others have attempted to restate the ontological argument. Kant's moral argument continues to enjoy popularity. The Neo-Thomists (e.g. Etienne Gilson, Jacques Maritain) have presented shrewder versions of Thomas's theistic proofs. And, of course, each time one of the older proof is presented anew, there are also new counterattacks.

I presume Barth's assessment would be that all these efforts to revive the proofs, and all the counterattacks on the revival of the proofs, are continued negative proof that every person has his or her religion, including the atheist, the communist, and the pantheist. But, in positive terms, this is not how God is known.

In staying with Calvin, Barth avoids the confusion, charge, and countercharge that accompany the debate over theistic proofs. With Calvin, Barth sees that the knowledge of God, the saving knowledge of God, the Christological knowledge of God, and the existence of God are all tied together and cannot be separated. He is concerned with special revelation, soteric (saving) revelation, the witness of Holy Scripture, and the centrality of the person of Christ and his Gospel. God's existence is not a matter of human proof, but of the divine self-demonstration, the divine self-attestation. We cannot (again with Calvin) separate the problem of the existence of God from the saving knowledge of God.

I think Barth has shown to the evangelicals the only realistic and biblical approach to the existence of God in the post-Enlightenment period of history. If he has done this, then his paradigm is of great service for evangelicals.

Note

1. Barth, *CD*, II/1.

15

Universalism

As NOTED EARLIER, one of the great documents of the Enlightenment was Gottfried Lessing's drama, *Nathan the Wise*. Except for the Hitler years, it has always played somewhere in Germany ever since its publication. The theme of the play is religious tolerance. It centers on three rings. The owner of the first ring was blessed of God and humanity. He was to give the ring to the son who seemed to best fulfill the meaning of the ring. The day came when a father had three sons each deserving of the ring. Therefore he had two perfect copies made of the original, so perfect that none could ever detect which was the original. The three rings were Judaism, Christianity, and Islam. Each bestowed the fundamental blessing of religion, which to Lessing was spirit and power. A debate over which son had the original ring was meaningless. So is the debate over which religion is the true religion.

Since the time of Lessing, we have learned much more of Africa and Asia, their religions and their philosophies. This knowledge has increased our problems. For example, what is the relationship of the Christian faith to the great civilizations of other continents and their ancient religions? What is the proper Christian response to the world population, which is growing far faster than the Christian population, so that the Christian population is becoming a smaller and smaller minority?

One response is to pick up some version of universalism, as pioneered by the great church father Origen (A.D. 185–254). If the species was lost in one man, it will be redeemed by one man, Christ—devil and all, Buddhists, Hindus, Muslims, and Animists!

In recent times, other alternatives have been suggested. One is the doctrine of the secret church. This doctrine teaches that God reaches people by the obvious means of the preaching of the Gospel but also by secret means unknown to the church. Hence there can well be millions of Buddhists, reached by secret means of God, who are in fact Christian. Another is the concept of the anonymous Christian, which teaches that all people who in some degree reflect Christian morality and spirituality are thereby Christians even though such a conviction does not rise to the level of consciousness. Thus in a large city such as London or Berlin there are certainly thousands of people who live according to Christian morality, yet who do not attend church nor confess the name of Christ. Hence they are anonymous Christians.

In both the nineteenth and twentieth centuries, the expression "the larger hope" has been used. This phrase expresses the belief that the Gospel will reach not only those who consciously confess it, but also somehow the larger world—in this life or the next. Or as some have put it, although some may not be evangelized in this world, they will be in the next. Such hope is based on I Peter 3:18–20. Still others avoid the issue by holding a doctrine of conditional immortality; namely, only believers are raised from the dead and live eternally. Another alternative is the doctrine of annihilation, which teaches that after due suffering the lost perish forever, an idea in the background of C. S. Lewis's *The Great Divorce*. Those who visit heaven and refuse to stay in heaven shrink away, losing their humanity until they are nothing.

As a class, evangelicals have been stoutly opposed to universalism. To them it is clear in a number of passages that there is a final separation of the saved and the lost. In the imagery of Augustine, the City of God and the City of Man finally separate, for all eternity. It is further argued that nothing cuts the nerve of evangelism and missions as does universalism. If nothing is really at stake in this life, why then should the church exert such energies in reaching the non-Christian populations of this world? It is also argued that liberal Christianity in all its forms, from Schleiermacher to Bultmann, is universalistic. Nobody is really saved or really lost in the theology of liberal Christianity.

Has Barth entered the lists for universalism or not? According to Brunner, he has; according to others, he has not. But something about Barth's "universalism" breaks with the discussion of the past, and that is what I wish to emphasize in this discussion.

First of all, Barth argues that no person can be a universalist, because only God knows whether all shall be saved or not. To affirm that God will save all is to affirm something none of us can know. It is true the other way, too! To affirm that God will only save some is a bit of knowledge none of us have. But Barth says, wouldn't it be nice if on Judgment Day grace should surprise us and save all![1]

Barth's final word on universalism is in *Church Dogmatics* (IV/3). He writes that we have no right to counter the Scriptural message that there is a final separation of the saved and the lost. No matter how our theology pushes us in that direction, we must not capitulate. But, then on the next page, he returns to the idea expressed in his *The Humanity of God:* God might surprise us! His grace is always beyond our calculation. He may save all!

Secondly, Barth's objectivity of salvation, in contrast to Bultmann's subjectivity of salvation, borders on universalism. This
requires some explanation. According to Barth, it was Schleiermacher who led Christian theology astray into liberal Christianity. Barth interprets Bultmann as the modern-day Schleiermacher, but with an orientation toward the philosophy of
Heidegger, not toward nineteenth-century romanticism. Barth
confesses that he has fought Bultmann with all his strength in
the later volumes of his *Church Dogmatics*,[2] even though he
does not name him, and in his essay *Rudolph Bultmann: An
Effort to Understand Him.*

Barth interprets both Schleiermacher and Bultmann as reducing the Christian message to a subjective religious experience. Schleiermacher reduced it to an experience of pious feeling; Bultmann reduced it to an existential commitment. Such a
reduction of Christianity to a subjective experience denies the
great objectivity of creation, revelation, the work of Christ, and
the experience of salvation. To overcome Bultmann's subjectivity, Barth defended the great objectivity of the work of Christ
and the objectivity of the experience of salvation. This amounted to overkill. It gave such a great objectivity to salvation that
it appeared to be universalism: so objective is the work of
Christ that it includes everybody!

A third aspect of Barth's universalism centers in the lordship of Christ. Barth believes rather literally that all power or
authority was given to Christ whether in heaven or on earth
(Matthew 28:18). Thus Christ is lord of all people, all nations,
in all centuries. Christ is lord of non-Christian—literally—as
well as Christian.

Barth also argues this point from Romans 13. The New Testament teaches that all authorities (*eksousia*) are under the
authority of Christ. With Cullmann, he believes that this includes political authorities. Hence Christ is lord of the state—
the so-called Christological foundation of the state. Accordingly, the authorities spoken of in Romans 13 are political authorities, and they are under the authority of Christ. Hence Christ's
universal lordship includes the state. Barth's concept of the

universal lordship of Christ also gives his theology a universalistic cast.

Another aspect of Barth's universalism relates to his view of evangelism and missions. From the standpoint of *de jure* (legal reckoning), all the world is reconciled to God in Christ. But *de facto* (as things actually are), only Christians know this and confess it. But in that all people are *de jure* Christians, the Christian is to treat all people as brothers and sisters. Hence Christian ethics, social ethics, or Christian humanitarianism is grounded in the presupposition that the whole world is *de jure* Christian. As seen in the discussion of humanism in this book, Barth's humanism is based on God's humanitarianism; and God's humanitarianism came to full exposure in the incarnation. This basis for Christian social ethics is new and radical.

If all the world is *de jure* Christian, then preaching, especially evangelistic preaching, asks people to recognize in fact (*de facto*) what they already are *de jure*. Barth believes that such an approach to evangelism and missions takes the unhealthy pressure off the evangelists and missionaries who feel so compelled to win converts.

Gerrit C. Berkouwer writes in *The Triumph of Grace in the Theology of Karl Barth* that Barth's view robs preaching of its seriousness, and the decision of faith of its meaningfulness. However, Barth never minimizes the difference between Christian and non-Christian, as seen in his lecture *Die Wirklichkeit des neuen Menschen* ("The Reality of the New Man"). The Christian church is made up of those people who have heard the call of the Gospel, have believed it, have experienced the new birth, and propose to live Christian lives. Barth does not convert the whole world into the church, as do many of the universalistic theologies of today. However, the weight of Berkouwer's objection is not to be overlooked, for it reflects the spiritual weakness of all universalisms.

The main weight of Barth's push for universalism is not about the old debate whether few be saved, or many be saved, or all be saved. His main concern is with the significance of the lives of people who are not Christian. Does the Gospel consign to meaninglessness all those people who have never heard it or never believed it? Are non-Christians the waste products of the plan of salvation?

This issue must be considered in the context of something mentioned earlier in this section. Billions of people have never heard the Gospel. There are easily more than two billion people alive today who have never heard a line of the Gospel and most likely never will. In terms of percentage, the church is a shrinking minority in the face of worldwide population growth. If significance for life is found only in Christ, then these millions and billions of lives are lived in insignificance.

The traditional matter of treating this problem was to make a distinction between creation and redemption. All people have significance before God in the order of creation. Insofar as they live their lives in the orders of creation (for example, state, family, education, commerce, farming, and medicine), their lives have significance. Whoever fulfills the orders of creation lives a meaningful life. There is a meaning to life for the non-Christian in the orders of creation, which Thielicke calls the penultimate meaning; only in Christ is the ultimate meaning. Such reflection may help soften the problem, but it hardly resolves it.

Another solution that has been offered is to say that all people eventually live to the glory of God. Those who become Christians praise the love and grace of God. Those who are lost reveal the perfect justice of God. Hence both the saved and the lost have significance because their lives glorify God. What this solution may gain in one direction, it loses in another. The person who is not a Christian is a tragic case, and it is always hard to rescue glory for God out of the tragedies of life.

Barth approaches the meaningfulness of the non-Christian person from another direction. Barth believes that Christ was the Last or Second Adam. As such, in his saving work he is the substitute for every single human being who has ever lived, is now alive or will yet live. Christ died for all; he was buried for all; he arose as Victor for all. All people are *de jure* ("on the books of God") justified. This means that Jesus Christ is related to all people: Europeans, Asians, Africans, Muslims, Animists, Buddhists, Hindus, Atheists. However, this relationship is se-cret—not obvious but nonetheless real. Jesus Christ is the secret meaning of every human life. Christians have experi-enced salvation and know this relationship. Non-Christians do not know it, but the fact remains unchanged.

The compassion of Barth in saving significance for every human life by relating it to God through Jesus Christ is cer-tainly commendable to every person of good Christian sensi-bilities. He does try to give meaning to billions of persons who under other premises would live completely meaningless lives. It is in this context that one must weigh Barth's push toward universalism.

Whether or not his solution is correct it is courageous. He faces an issue that is so staggering that most of us gloss it over to avoid the uncomfortable experience of thinking about it. Maybe such suggestions are the ways Christians soften a truth but resolve nothing. But it is better to feel the problem than not to feel it; and it is more Christian to suffer some periods of intense spiritual agony than to gloss over the problem. Wheth-er Barth has led the church out of this theological thicket re-mains to be seen from further theological reflection.

Barth cannot help us in the matter of universalism if we expect to find in him a peaceful resolution of the universal love of God and the fate of the human race in that Last Day. His distinction between *de facto* and *de jure* may be nothing more than a convenient fiction.

His help for evangelical theology comes from other direc-tions. We can learn more of the comprehensive lordship of Christ from Barth's theology. We can become aware to the sur-prises of grace that might be in store for all of us. But most of all, Barth warns us not to write off in any cavalier way the fate of billions of people who have never heard of Christ or of future billions who never will. Or, to put it another way, if God's compassion has been opened up to us in our knowledge of Christ, that compassion should reach out to all humanity. Few things are more un-Christian than a juridical, stony response to the problem of the lostness of billions of human beings.

Notes

1. Karl Barth, *The Humanity of God*, trans. J. N. Thomas and T. Weiser (Richmond, Va.: John Knox Press, 1960), pp. 61–62.
2. Barth, *CD*, IV/1, pp. vii, ix.

16

Humanism

HUMANISM IS ONE of those many terms that we know what they mean until we are asked to define them. There is the classical humanism of the Greeks, which in turn inspired the Renaissance humanism. The Enlightenment is understood as the continuation of the Renaissance after the interlude of the Reformation, so it too is classified as a period of humanism. The twentieth century has been marked by humanism also especially in the use of such terms as neohumanism and Third-Wave Humanism. It is really difficult to use the singular any more, for humanism now means a cluster of humanisms.

In the history of European and Western culture since the beginning of the eighteenth century, different elements of humanism gradually replaced the Christian assumptions of Western culture. For example, under the influence of thinkers like Hobbes, Locke, and Rousseau the state has come to be understood as a purely human arrangement (for example, a social contract), rather than an institution founded by God on equal parity with the church, as in the political thought of Christian theologians from Augustine to Luther and Calvin. Morality was separated from religion, and ethics was declared to be founded solely on philosophical analysis, whether it be Kant's categorical imperative or the utilitarianism of Bentham. New humanistic theories of education began in the Enlightenment, especially in Jean-Jacques Rousseau's *Émile.* Hugo Grotius's work on international law was another movement in founding human order on human arrangements rather than on divine law. Answers to philosophical questions were not to be found in divine revelation but in human reason. This cluster of humanisms eventually replaced the Christian assumptions of Western culture much the way chemicals slowly and systematically replace wood fiber in petrified wood.

Christian cultural assumptions did not evaporate with the Enlightenment. The Christian momentum of a millennium could not be lost that readily. But the momentum has been greatly weakened. Humanisms of the past (Greek and Renaissance) did not set up a conflict between humanism and religion. The Renaissance humanists were all Catholics. But humanism since the Enlightenment has become consciously secular. It advocates life without God, community without the church, and philosophy without revelation. It has also added humanitarianism to its humanism. The humanists of recent times wish to eliminate all suffering, all oppression, and all wars from the human scene. The humanists are utilitarians in wanting the greatest good for the greatest number. In recent times, the welfare state has arisen, and its connection with humanism is more than accidental.

However, the twentieth century has been the scene of the greatest embarrassment for humanism. Along with the greatest propaganda for humanism, we have experienced the most inhuman century of the human race. The charter of the United Nations reads as a very humanistic document. But in the twentieth century we have been faced with two world wars, the dropping of atomic bombs, and the emergence of oppressive, brutal totalitarian states, both of Marxist ideology and the military. Furthermore, the Western nations are experiencing a staggering rise of crime and terrorism.

No matter how brutal the wars, no matter how cruel the governments, no matter how oppressive the systems, it paradoxically remains the common assumption in the twentieth century that all people, all nations, and all governments are to be guided by humanism with its humanitarian principles.

---∽---

Evangelicals have a stake in the current discussion about humanism. This stake is brought out in the famous Babbitt-Eliot exchange over humanism. Irving Babbitt was a learned and influential professor at Harvard (1865-1933). He was a strong defender of neohumanism, which he propounded in his book *Democracy and Leadership* (1924). The poet T. S. Eliot was a student of Babbitt's at Harvard, and an admirer of him, but he criticized Babbitt's version of neohumanism.

In a critical essay, Eliot finds fault with Babbitt's neohumanism at a number of points. First of all, it is a degenerate form of orthodox Christianity. Eliot believed that as Christianity was diluted from orthodoxy to liberal Christianity, it ended in humanism, neither of which (i.e., liberal Christianity and humanism) had the internal resources to sustain themselves. André Dumas cites French essayist Denis de Rougemont as an unexpected witness to Eliot's opinion:

> Once Denis de Rougemont, after having remarked upon the Thomism of Dante, the Calvinism of Rembrandt, the Lutheranism of Bach, and the Puritanism of Milton, noted the sterility of the liberal Protestantism of the nineteenth and twentieth centuries, for it did not inspire any artist, musician, poet, or creative philosopher because it did not have any clear and firm requirement and because it did not fix any limit which would be at the same time a stimulus and a guide.[1]

The second criticism was that humanism had become a religion, but as a religion it had nothing to sustain it nor counter strong adverse forces. It was at best the belief of a few intellectuals, who could sustain it out of their own resources, but as a religion for the larger populace it was hopeless.

Critics of Eliot's attack on Babbitt said that Eliot forced one to choose between humanism and religion. Or to put it otherwise, humanism and religion were mutually exclusive choices. When Eliot heard of that criticism of his first essay, he wrote a second essay to correct it. The last thing Eliot wanted to do was to give the impression that he was against the values of classical humanism, Renaissance humanism, and current humanism. In this second essay, Eliot made a distinction between humanism as a set of attitudes that each and every Christian ought to approve, and humanism as a substitute religion, which he still opposed. He believed that the root of humanism must be religion, for humanism could not sustain itself. But to imagine that a Christian must choose between humanism and religion was erroneous.

At this point, the evangelical enters the debate. Sometimes evangelical condemnations of the "world" give the impression that one must choose either Christianity or humanism. Or in evangelical condemnations of "worldly amusements," the impression can be given that Christians are anticultural. Or, in condemning all heathen to total ignorance of God and to being lost, it can give the impression that evangelicals are less than humane. And certainly there are dark judgments about humanity in the Christian doctrines of depravity, divine wrath, and the coming judgment. Is evangelical theology opposed to culture, against humanism (in its finer definition), and against the humanitarian impulse?

Evangelicals live in a culture that has substituted its humanism for the Christian presuppositions in all aspects of life— law, medicine, education, and politics. It is a serious question whether evangelical theology has both a humane and humanitarian impulse in it. For this reason, we turn to Barth's version of Christian humanism.

———— ∞ ————

A number of International Conferences of Geneva have been held in which outstanding scholars or thinkers of Europe spend ten days in discussing some very current issue. The results are then published as *Rencontres Internationales de Genève*. Barth was invited to the 1949 conference, which discussed humanism ("Pour un nouvel humanisme"). It included Marxists, existentialists (Jaspers), scientists (Haldane), and theologians (Barth and the Roman Catholic Maydieu). In a booklet, *Humanismus,* Barth presents the brief talk he gave at the conference and his report of the conference given at Zurich, February 2, 1951. It is also interesting that in the brief article on humanism in the fifteenth edition of the Encyclopaedia Britannica, the only name mentioned of a twentieth-century person is that of Karl Barth.

Barth observed that the conference could not define humanism. It offered definitions here and there, but none were substantial enough to win any kind of approval. One definition suggested was that humanism was to respect everybody else's humanism. That is circular definition par excellence. Another oddity was the claim of the Marxists that only Marxism offers the true humanism. If there is any country guilty of the most serious crimes of inhumanity, it is Russia, as graphically described in Aleksandr Solzhenitsyn's *The Gulag Archipelago.* Still another oddity was Jasper's speech describing our terrible world and yet hoping that out of the current world chaos a new humanism will arise.

Barth and Eliot are also of the same mind that humanism does not have the power to sustain itself. Eliot called it a religion; Barth called it an ideology. Whether religion or ideology, it is weak if not impotent before the evils of the world. Barth also pointed out that as much as Christians may differ over the concept of humanism, nevertheless as a people they have far more unity about the interpretation of humanism than do any of the non-Christian options. Furthermore, Barth observed that there is no grace in humanism, whether Marxist or existential (e.g., Heidegger and Sartre). Where there is no grace, there is no forgiveness of the past, no sources of renewal when all seems lost, and no power to confront the powerful evils of society.

Barth bases his Christian humanism on the humanitarianism of God. He uses various expressions that really do lose something in translation: *die Menschenfreundlichkeit Gottes,*

"God's friendliness toward people"; *die Humanismus Gottes,* "the humanism of God"; *der menschenfreundliche Gott,* "the God who is friendly toward people." It is the decision of the triune God to be the God, Lord, and Shepherd of humanity. It is a decision of pure grace, for it is not based on a necessity in God or on human deserving.

Historically, God's humanism (or Christian humanism) takes place in the incarnation. The incarnation means several things. It reveals God's love for humanity and God's identification with humanity. The story from Bethlehem to the Cross reveals how God's Son totally identified himself with the human burden. The cross in particular reveals how God's Son took up our burden, guilt, and sin, and in his own body and in his own death bore them away.

Dorothy L. Sayers caught this notion of the humanity of God and expressed it in her own remarkable way:

> What does the Church think of Christ? The Church's answer is categorical and uncompromising, and it is this: That Jesus Bar-Joseph, the carpenter of Nazareth, was in fact and in truth, and in the most exact and literal sense of the words, the God "by whom all things were made." His body and brain were those of a common man; His personality was the personality of God, so far as that personality could be expressed in human terms. He was not a kind of demon or fairy pretending to be human; He was in every respect a genuine living man. He was not merely a man so good as to be "like God"—He *was* God.
>
> Now, this is not just a pious commonplace; it is not commonplace at all. For what it means it this, among other things: that for whatever reason God chose to make man as he is— limited and suffering and subject to sorrows and death—He had the honesty and the courage to take His own medicine. Whatever game He is playing with His creation, He has kept His own rules and played fair. He can exact nothing from man that He has not exacted from Himself. He has Himself gone through the whole of human experience, from the trivial irritations of family life and the cramping restrictions of hard work and lack of money to the worst horrors of pain and humiliation, defeat, despair, and death. When He was a man, He

played the man. He was born in poverty and died in disgrace and thought it well worth while.[2]

A number of secondary theses accompany the humanism based on the humanitarianism of God. Barth's humanism forms a solid basis for defending human rights and human worth. It reveals that Jesus Christ is the true person, the real human being, and therefore we see in Jesus Christ the person we are all intended to be. Christian humanism does not compete with all our other knowledge of humanity. There is much in humanism that Christians may approve. But it must all be seen in the perspective of the humanism of God if it is to be seen in the right light.

The humanism of God forbids that we should be pessimists or skeptics or that we should resign ourselves to the tragic. Christian humanism has its own teachings on how it is to work. We are promised the help of the Holy Spirit. We are given the motivation of faith and love. Christian humanism is a living, practical, working faith.

In summary, Barth gives an invitation (in his lecture at Geneva). He invites his listeners to repent (*tut Busse!*), to be converted (*Bekehrung*), and to believe the Gospel (*das Evangelium*). Furthermore, Barth is convinced that humanists greatly underestimate the powers of evil that work against the human race, and that their faith in humanism is at best a half-hearted effort lacking any real moral force. He ends by remarking that the only humanism that has endured the centuries is Christian humanism, and it is most likely the only humanism that will survive this current epoch. The only enduring humanism is that which is based on the incarnation. He concludes with the words of the Nicene Creed: *"et incarnatus est de Spiritu Sancto ex Maria virgine et homo factus est"* ("and was made flesh by the Holy Spirit and the virgin Mary, and became man").

Humanisms are here to stay. Different humanisms and different aspects of humanism are now the foundation of our le-

gal systems, our educational systems, and our common assumptions of civilization. Evangelicals need an articulate
understanding of humanisms if they are to live perceptively in
a humanistic society. Historically, evangelicals have been part
of a broad Christian humanism, perhaps best stated by Roman
Catholic theologians.

Barth has set out in his own radical way a new basis for
humanism—the humanitarianism of God. Of course, Barth has
not said anything new here, but he has said it in a new context
and in a radical manner. Barth embraces the humanism of
John 3:16 in the context of the modern effort to define the new
humanism. Also, Barth's humanism is not forced to deny any
virtue or truth in the competing humanisms or other studies of
humanity. Barth's humanism has the virtue of being a paradigm for evangelicals. If they do not like Barth's paradigm,
they at least know from studying Barth what the shape must
be of any evangelical interpretation of humanism.

Notes

1. André Dumas, "Theologie et Humanisme," in Jean-Jacques von Allmen, ed., *Hommage et Reconnaisance* [Recueil de travaux publiés à l'occasion du soixantième anniversaire de Karl Barth] (Neuchatel: Delachaux
   et Niestlé, 1946), p. 201.
2. Dorothy L. Sayers, *Creed or Chaos* (London: Religious Book Club, 1947),
   pp. 1–2.

17

Christological Eschatology

THE ENLIGHTENMENT DISCARDED the common Christian eschatological beliefs about the return of Christ, the end of the world, final judgment, heaven and hell. The writers of this period were not, however, indifferent about the question of the course of history. Significantly, at the end of the Enlightenment appeared Hegel's great attempt to write a philosophy of history. But the common eschatological tradition of the Christian church was rejected. History now had other interpretations and meanings than the traditional Christian ones.

There was also an attack on traditional eschatology from within the church. This attack was mounted in the name of biblical criticism. The denial of supernatural revelation implied the rejection of historic Christian eschatology. Not until the end of the nineteenth century was the full weight of pressure against traditional eschatology felt. The acme of the development was the many works on Jewish and Christian eschatology by the world's leading expert on these themes, Robert Henry Charles (1855–1931).

In a word, the Enlightenment both within and outside the church initiated the downfall of Christian eschatology, a task thoroughly completed at the end of the nineteenth century.

For example, Dante's *Divine Comedy*, having lost its eschatological significance, became solely a poem for literary research.

————··❦··————

Despite the Enlightenment, however, eschatology did not disappear. The Enlightenment and critical biblical scholarship had no impact on evangelical pastors and believers who persisted in their traditional eschatology. Eschatology also persisted among all the theological and biblical scholars of an orthodox persuasion who also retained their hold on their traditional eschatology.

Nor could religious liberal theology totally avoid eschatology. It retained a measure of eschatological thought in its doctrine of the kingdom of God and of the immortality of the soul. The kingdom of God was to progressively spread into all the world in the sense that more and more of human social, political, and economic life would be governed by the biblical concepts of love and justice. With reference to the immortality of the soul, liberal theology virtually reproduced the version of Plato in the *Phaedo*. The argument considered a bodily resurrection a crass materialistic concept of the future life. But in liberal Christianity, traditional eschatology was dead in the water.

Bernhard Weiss and Albert Schweitzer demonstrated that eschatological thinking was not something at the edge of Jesus' teachings but was stage center. Jesus could not be properly interpreted if the eschatological element of his teaching were omitted. Hence there have been a number of efforts to retain eschatological motifs without retreating to traditional church eschatology.

Paul Althaus's idealized eschatology and Charles H. Dodd's realized eschatology have much in common in affirming that eschatological concepts describe the current spiritual condition of humanity rather than end-time events. If the kingdom of God is truly here, then the *eschaton* (a Greek word) is here. According to Paul Tillich, eternal life is limited to our experience in this lifetime. Eternal life is the dimension of spirit in our lives; it is the living of life in true Christian authenticity. But death is the end of the line for all people. Bultmann's view is that the eschatological is the sense the Christian has that the *kerygma* ("the gospel") is given of God, not created by human imagination. In process theology, our immortality consists in being eternally remembered by God.

Other writers, such as Oscar Cullmann, Jürgen Moltmann, and Wolfhart Pannenberg, try to keep eschatology in touch with history. The Christian hope has to be more than an attitude (to which it had been reduced in Bultmann's theology). In addition, the apocalyptic elements in Holy Scripture have been more positively evaluated (see Walter Schmithals, *The Apocalyptic Movement*).

These remarks are intended to give a minimal overview about eschatology in our time. For a more detailed survey, see Hans Schwarz, *On the Way to the Future: A Christian View of Eschatology in the Light of Current Trends in Religion, Philosophy and Science.*

Fundamentalism has its roots in the nineteenth century. Although some differences of opinion arise over the factors that generated it, there is no question that millenarianism was one such factor. David A. Rausch has done the most concentrated research on this aspect of the origin of fundamentalism in his book, *Zionism Within Early American Fundamentalism: 1878– 1918.* However, he does move beyond the 1918 date and comments on the issues in current times.

Although in the first famous five fundamentals of the Niagara Conference (1895) the millennium is not mentioned, nevertheless all the important people of that time in the movement were millenarians. Eventually this millenarianism was spelled out as premillennial dispensationalism. Eschatological thinking was at a low ebb in academic theology, but it was heating up to the higher registers among the fundamentalists.

This movement was caused by many historical factors. The American evangelist Dwight L. Moody was advised by dispensational writers, and when he institutionalized his movement into a school and a printing press, his program incorporated dispensationalism. Bible Institutes were founded across the country, teaching dispensational theology as orthodoxy. The *Scofield Reference Bible*, with a dispensational theology embodied in its notes, sold millions of copies. Smaller movements that arose and had no particular eschatology latched on to the already available dispensational eschatology. The dispensational press published such widely distributed books of such popular Bible teachers as William B. Blackstone's *Jesus Is Coming* and Cyrus I. Scofield's *Rightly Dividing the Word of Truth*.

Philip Edgcumbe Hughes makes an important observation in his book *Interpreting Prophecy*. He comments that dispensationalists claim that only their theology is an adequate bulwark against all forms of liberal Christianity. The fundamentalists in many instances challenged liberal theology, both within their own denominations and in American church life. Hence in the mind of pastors and laity it was an easy step to identify fundamentalism with orthodoxy. And then the further step was taken: if fundamentalists were dispensationalists and premillennialists, then those positions too must be part of orthodoxy.

The founding of the Moody Bible Institute as a center of premillennial and dispensational theology was the beginning. At present dispensational theology is taught as standard, orthodox theology in many Bible colleges, Christian liberal arts colleges, and theological seminaries. A continuous movement among dispensationalists has been the holding of prophetic conferences, during which a number of speakers lecture on prophetic themes. There have also emerged prophetic specialists, who make their living by lecturing and preaching on prophetic themes.

As Rausch documents it in his book, dispensationalism is also Zionism. Zionism is the belief that modern Israel has title deeds to the land of Palestine based on promises in the Old Testament. Dispensationalists believe that modern Israel is therefore right in establishing its own state in Palestine. In recent political conflicts in the Middle East, dispensationalists consistently side with Israel against the Arab states.

The popularity of dispensational fundamentalism came to its most awesome success with the publication of Hal Lindsey's *The Late Great Planet Earth*. This book has sold millions of copies and continues to sell in the supermarkets in America. It was also made into a movie, distributed nationally. James Barr says part of the reason for such success is that so many people confuse Lindsey's book with science fiction.[1] Similarly, as Hughes noted, no doubt thousands of pastors and hundreds of thousands of the laity think that traditional Christianity, orthodoxy, the faith once and for all delivered to the saints, and dispensational fundamentalism are all one and the same.

One other observation is in order. In reading much dispensationalist literature, one encounters claims that amount to sinless perfection in biblical intepretation. Writers of this persuasion state that they are reading the Word of God for exactly what it says, or that they are reading it with pure eyes that have not been contaminated with traditional views of eschatology; or that, not having had academic theological education, they can read the Scriptures unclouded by human opinion. Lewis Sperry Chafer himself claimed that, not having had academic training in theology, he was free to interpret the Scriptures with unclouded objectivity.

The fundamentalists' belief that they read the prophetic parts of Holy Scripture with pure objectivity runs contrary to their doctrines of original sin and total depravity. It is remarkable that with reference to prophetic interpretation they claim freedom from the influence of depravity, while in their doctrine of sin they maintain traditional doctrines of original sin and total depravity.

Historically informed evangelicals are caught between the millstones. They agree with Paul in I Corinthians 15 that the Christian Gospel not only looks back to the cross and resurrection of Christ but also looks forward to the return of Christ and to the bodily resurrection of the believer. Furthermore, they agree with Paul that if we do not have such a hope we are of all people the most miserable. Therefore they cannot agree with the discarding of historic eschatology by the Enlightenment and its contemporary children.

On the other hand, historically informed evangelicals cannot accept the fanciful projections of the future one finds in dispensationalism, which charts out the future in amazing detail and with all confidence, as if dispensationalists had already lived through the events and were recording them as history experienced. People familiar with the history of interpretation and of millennial speculation know all the imponderables in the dispensational system. In view of Eastern Orthodox, Roman Catholic, Lutheran, Reformed, and Anglican theology, dispensationalism's sharp division of the church and Israel, each going its own unique course through history into eternity, is a remarkable piece of theological heresy. However these groups may have differed, they were united in the great unities of Augustine's *City of God*. Augustine unified the people of God in both Testaments (Israel and the church) as the one people of the City of God. He unified the Scriptures with the notion that Christ was the hidden content of the Old Testament and the revealed content of the New. And he unified theology around the themes of creation, fall, sin, redemption, and Jesus Christ.

With its seven dispensations, eight covenants, and the absolute difference between Israel and the church, dispensationalism fractures the Augustinian unities. The City of God is fractured into Israel and the church. The unity of Scripture is fractured into seven dispensations and eight covenants. The unity of theology is fractured into a traditional body of material and a special dispensational body of material.

The fifth volume of *Church Dogmatics* was intended to be on the theme of eschatology or final redemption. Although it was never written, Barth said his position could be guessed from what he had written. Barth discusses Christ as the lord of time and in that discussion gives the essence of his eschatology.[2] In a phrase, it is *consistent Christological eschatology.*

Permit a personal reference. As a young Christian, I was thoroughly exposed to the premillennial dispensational system and its charts. I not only patiently studied, with great reverence, the *Scofield Reference Bible* and its notes but time and time again I leafed through the charts in Clarence Larkin's *Dispensational Truth.* At the Bible class I attended as much as time allowed, I was faced with a huge dispensational chart stretching across the entire platform, sketching the history of events from Alpha Eternity to Omega Eternity. To me, eschatology was primarily the listing of events that would run their course in serial order.

This notion Barth challenges to the core. Jesus Christ is an eschatological person. He is eschatological in that he was raised from the dead; he walked around this earth for forty days in the body of eternity; he ascended to the right hand of God; he now rules; and he shall return again. There is meaning to eschatological events only as there is the eschatological person. One reason so much dispensationalist literature reads so oddly is that it is not adequately tied in with Christological thought. The bearing of the eschatological charts on essential biblical and Christological materials is remote. The events in the dispensational scheme are presented as if they had a self-contained meaning and self-contained substance (as in the wild and grotesque speculations of the meaning of 666 and the identity of the man of sin).

Barth understands the preexistence of Christ (as he appears in the Old Testament), the incarnation, the crucifixion, the resurrection, the ascension, the heavenly reign, and the return of Christ to be one event. They are not one event in the sense of happening at the same time. Rather, each event implicates the other events in such a manner that no one event can be separated from any other. They are a unified sequence that cannot suffer division.

A famous preacher was asked what he felt about the second coming. His reply was that he was so busy preaching about the first coming he had not come around to preaching on the second coming. According to Barth, this is an idiotic remark. Unless there is a second coming of Christ, the first coming hangs suspended with no purpose, no goal, no *telos*.

The second coming is an event of redemption. When one reads typical dispensational books about the signs of the second coming and the battle of Armageddon, one has a good reason to wonder what has happened to eschatology. The return of Christ as the final event of redemption has been turned into an odd political, sociological, economical this-world event. In fact, such an interpretation loses the eschatological dimension, for it has been reduced to a this-world event among other this-world events. But, even more serious, the second coming has been cut off from its natural location in the plan of redemption and has taken on all the characteristics that in other books by sectarians would be branded as "cultic millenarianism." It is very symptomatic that dispensationalists are embarrassed by hyperdispensationalism and various forms of Adventism, for these movements are closely related to millenarianism.

Furthermore, Barth does not believe that the second coming should be hushed up and interpreted as if it coincided with the quiet demise of the world, with the mysterious disappearance of Christians into heaven. In fact, he chided the Congregation of the Sacred Office (the one in charge of sacred doctrine) for stating that the glorious, visible return of Christ is not a certain teaching of the New Testament.[3] According to Barth, the resurrection of Christ makes the visible return of Christ the greatest certainty in the New Testament. Whatever the Roman Catholic Church may have thought to have gained by such a decision, Barth thinks it takes the stuffings out of the second coming—it "de-eschatologizes" the second coming.[4]

In a letter, someone asked Barth how he defined eternal life. He answered by defining eternal life and then relating it to the second coming:

> We thus wait and hope, even in view of our death, for our manifestation with Him, with Jesus Christ who was raised again

from the dead, in the glory of not only the judgment but also the grace of God. The new thing will be that the cover of tears, death, suffering, crying, and pain that now lies over our present life will be lifted, that the decree of God fulfilled in Jesus Christ will stand before our eyes, and that it will be the subject not only of our deepest shame but also of our joyful thanks and praise.[5]

Something should be said of Barth's view of the continued existence of Israel.

In most millenarian eschatology, the millennum is interpreted as the time when all the kingdom promises made to Israel are fulfilled. These Old Testament texts are joined to Revelations 20:1–10 and hence filled out to mean the personal reign of Christ on Earth for a thousand years. Such millennial views have been found intermittently in the history of the Christian church from the second century to the present.

In *The City of God*, Augustine identified the City of God with all the redeemed of all the ages, commencing with Adam and following through to the end of history in the Book of Revelation. Israel and the church in historical sequence are the one people of God, the New Israel (see Galatians 6:16). Strong millenarian beliefs again sprang up at the time of the Reformation. However, both the Lutherans and the Reformed stayed with Augustine's concept of the one people of God, comprising Israel and the church. Furthermore, the two traditions stated in their creeds that there could be no millennium based on the revival of Jewish hopes.

The Augustinian premise adds up to the conclusion that after the coming of Christ there is no future for Israel as such. Jew and Gentile alike are to believe in Christ and so form the Christian church.

However, the millennial beliefs stirred up during the Reformation persisted intermittently from the time of the Reformation to the present (see the excellent brief survey by E. Bradtke and A. C. Beckwith, "Millennium, Millenarianism").[6] Millenarian views became strong in the late nineteenth century and have persisted into the twentieth century. They have been much reinforced by the founding of the state of Israel in the aftermath of World War II.

The Augustinian view (generally called *amillennialism*) has been criticized as being too allegorical in regards to the Scriptures and too Platonic in its view of the relationship of the church militant in heaven and the suffering-pilgrim church on Earth. The millenarian view has been criticized for interpreting the Bible with a crass literalism.

Is there a third option in this matter? Barth says yes. He does not believe that revelation is totally private. Rather, revelation has left three visible signs in the world to indicate to the world that revelation has occurred, that God has acted in human history for the salvation of the world. Those three signs are Israel, the church, and Holy Scripture.

Israel persists in history because God will let none of his signs disappear. Israel is a sign to all the world that God did elect this nation to be his people and to write the Old Testament; that there is such a thing as divine revelation; and that there is such a thing as salvation history. The emergence of the state of Israel is not a sign that millennial promises are near to fulfilment. On the unity of the people of God, Barth is one with Augustine and Calvin. But the emergence of the state of Israel is one more indication in world history that God will not let this sign of his revelation and salvation disappear.

When the city fathers of Basel proposed a great celebration in their city, Barth protested because the Jews were not invited. The Jews, he reminded them, are the brothers of our Lord. The relationship between synagogue and church differs from the relationship among any other of the world's religions.

Barth therefore offers us an understanding of Israel that does not involve us in the problems of millenarianism or in the skittishness of much amillennial thought over the question of Israel and her persistence in world history.

Barth's manner of handling Eschatology is a good paradigm for evangelicals. It shows the proper relationship of the eschatological person Christ to the eschatological events. He does not want the person without events, for he scolds Moltmann for speaking of eschatology apart from events of eschatology.[7] How meaningless are so many works on the millennium and other aspects of eschatology that discuss these events as if they had meaning, substance, and importance apart from Jesus Christ.

Furthermore, Barth's eschatology will not surrender the "eventness" of the eschatological. Barth does not dilute eschatology, as do Bultmann, Tillich, and process theologians. In an exceptionally sharp sentence, Barth says that if a theologian has no interest in the risen, reigning, and returning Christ he or she ought to forget about Christianity because that is what Christianity is all about. Unless there is a real eschatological event centering on Jesus Christ at the end of history, history has no meaning. If a theologian cuts off the return of Christ from theology then he or she trivialized history and his or her own theology.

By anchoring eschatology in Christology, Barth gives it its right rationale. In that Hal Lindsey is classed among other evangelicals, his book *The Late Great Planet Earth* which has received such negative—even scathing—reviews in theological journals, is a burden to all who fall under the caption of evangelical. Barth's eschatology is not involved in speculations about world politics and world economics, as if we could not believe in the return of Christ unless the world situation assented to it. There is a rationale to Barth's Christological eschatology, unlike much dispensational eschatology that anchors itself so sturdily to a given sequence of events that, as mentioned before, can have only the most tenuous connections with Christology. Barth's eschatology does not pledge us to a speculative system of events and to esoteric interpretations of contemporary events. Barth's discussion of eschatology has many pages of the exegesis of eschatological passages. He does not fly his theology high over the texts of Scripture. Unless one reads the pages of the *Church Dogmatics* itself, one will have no idea of Barth's extensive use of Scripture in the exposition of his ideas on eschatology.

Notes

1. James Barr, *Fundamentalism* (Philadelphia: Westminster Press, 1977), pp. 206–207.
2. Barth, *CD*, III/2.
3. Barth, *CD*, III/2, p. 510.
4. Barth, *CD*, III/2, p. 511.
5. Karl Barth, *Letters: 1961-1968*, trans. Goeffrey Bromiley (Grand Rapids, Mich.: Eerdmans, 1981), no. 4, p. 9.
6. E. Bradtke and A. C. Beckwith, "Millennium, Millenarianism," in *Schaff–Herzog Encyclopedia of Religious Knowledge*, vol. 7, pp. 374–378.
7. Barth, *Letters: 1961-1968*, pp. 174–176.

18

The Laughing Barth

BARTH WAS KNOWN among the theologians as a humorist. Especially in his later years, there was never a lecture in his Basel lecture hall that was not punctuated a number of times with a touch of humor. "Basel humor" had become a common expression. What has humor to do with theology?

Humor is an interesting psychological phenomenon that yet awaits full psychological explanation. As both Henri Bergson and Karl Barth have said, the human being is the only animal that laughs. Humor has a wide range of expression from the barbed humor of masked hostility to the innocent humor of the circus clown. There is sick humor, and there is healthy humor. We are concerned with the latter.

People who have studied the psychology and sociology of humor have said that the function of humor is to remind us of our common humanity, especially in its weakness and stupidity. Humor reminds us that we are not gods nor goddesses. It has also been observed that dictators and fanatics lack a sense of humor. Dictators and fanatics have classified themselves among the gods and goddesses and therefore cannot tolerate reminders of their humanity in its weakness and stupidity.

A second function of humor is that it adds to a healthy objectivity in our perceptions and therefore helps keep things in their perspective. Art Buchwald has had such a distinguished career as a humorist because he has brought such a healing touch of objectivity to the national political scene, where the temptation is so great for politicians to pose as gods and for fanatics to pose as prophets.

Humor is necessary in theology for the same reasons it is necessary in common life and in politics. Theologians can pose as gods and can become fanatics. It is a particular disease of theology for its practitioners to take themselves too seriously. In explaining the divine majesty, it is a common temptation to presume that oneself has some of that majesty. If dictators and fanatics have no sense of humor, neither have theologians who unwittingly slip into the role of either dictator or fanatic. Beware of theologians without a sense of humor!

Humor in theology serves the function of reminding every theologian that he or she is a human being performing a very human task. One delightful aspect of Busch's biography of Barth is learning about Barth's ever-present sense of humor. Barth never lost touch with common human experience nor with his own common humanity. What a contrast between the laughing Barth and some of his stern, serious, grim, humorless critics!

Barth never wearies of reminding his readers that theology is a human task. Even though it is in service of the Word of God, in the service of the serious business of preaching, and in the service of the most important of all subject matters, it is nevertheless a very human task that must be done over and over again. We must never lost sight of our humanity even in theology. On one occasion, Barth wrote very critically against people whose whole lives were preoccupied with religion and the church. His point was that if people have no concern for art, literature, drama, sports, or politics, then they have lost touch with humanity. And to lose touch with humanity is to disdain our common humanity and have a pathological understanding of it. To become totally religious is to lose sight of the fact that every human life is a pilgrimage, including our own.

Humor is a prime means of breaking us away from the introversion of life totally into religion, totally into theology, totally into the church.

———————∽———————

Heinrich Vogel approaches the humor of Barth from a different perspective than the one we have presented.[1] He approaches Barth from the standpoint of comedy as technically defined in literature. In drama, if the plot has a good ending it is comedy, and if it has a sad ending it is tragedy. The symbol of the stage is the two masks: one smiling for comedy and one frowning for tragedy.

In that the Gospel is good news, it is comedy. Barth is not a jokester, for the jokester engages in playing funny tricks. If Barth were a jokester, his God would be the biggest jokester of them all. Barth's humor is based on the good news of the Gospel, and therefore he can be the smiling and laughing Barth, for all will end well in God's purposes in Jesus Christ. Therefore Barth's humor is not sick humor but "refreshing, human, natural and healthy."[2]

That element in Barth's theology I would not deny. It coincides with Barth's affirmation that theology is the happiest of sciences and that the theologian with a long face should give up theology. Theology is also the most beautiful of sciences.

I am looking at Barth from the standpoint of the psychological and social function of humor. The function of healthy humor is to remind us of our common humanity and for what it is. In the exaggerations of the clowns, we are really seeing ourselves and sharing in the fact that we too, in our limited, finite, and errant human natures, are clowning our way through life.

Evangelical theology needs a touch of humor to remind it that it too is a very human activity. Only in humor can evangelical theology avoid the humorless theological dictator and theological fanatic. If we have no sense of humor in our theology, we then take ourselves with an inhuman seriousness.

How funny it is to hear some prophetic expert speak of future events as if he himself (or herself) had lived through them and was reporting them as history! How funny to hear a lecture on the inerrancy of Scripture by a lecturer who presumes his or her argument is as inerrant as the thesis! How comical is a sermon in which the preacher attempts to persuade us that God causes all events in the universe! Even this one? How hard it is to resist a smile when we are told that infants can believe but on all other points of their little lives remain infants! And, it may be politely asked of the Calvinists, if the Arminians are so wicked why did God decree that they exist? And of course there is the classic in which the preacher with a wig, false teeth, glasses, and a wooden leg invites us to a healing meeting!

Evangelical theology needs a touch of humor. It needs a touch of humor to enable it to always distinguish between the given-ness of the Word of God and theology, which is a human product. We need a touch of humor to perpetually remind us that there is always a measurable distance between our human efforts to state what we find in the Word of God and what is truly there. Humor in theology does not mean we take theology with less seriousness. Barth took it with maximum seriousness and produced the largest theology in the history of the church. But humor prevented him (and can prevent evangelical theology) from taking theology with pathological seriousness.

One other aspect of the healthy service of humor arises in theological discussion. One cannot really have a dialogue with a fanatic or an ideologue. The person with a theology or apologetics or a given piece of theology that he or she defends with maximum seriousness and at all costs and at every occasion is a fanatic, an ideologue. One cannot have a true dialogue with such a person. There is a very perceptive line in the play *Inherit the Wind* in which one character says to another, "Lady, when you lose your power to laugh, you lose your power to think straight."[3] Whoever has become humorless in theology has lost his or her ability to think straight. Pathological seriousness distorts one's power to reason correctly. The clown no longer reminds such a person that in all life including theological life, he or she is fallible and errant, and at times tragically stupid and at other times comically stupid. If we understand clowns, we will never make that fateful identification of our theology and our apologetics with the final Word of God.

Notes

1. Heinrich Vogel, "Der lachende Barth" ["The Laughing Barth"], in *Antwort*, pp. 64–171.
2. Ibid., p. 171.
3. Jerome Lawrence and Robert E. Lee, *Inherit the Wind* (New York: Bantam Books, 1960), p. 45.

Reservations About Barth's Theology

Barth repeatedly asserted that theology was never a completed task. All theologies were provisional, including his own. He thought it providential that he was not able to finish the *Church Dogmatics* (in the tradition of Thomas Aquinas!), for that was a witness to the provisional nature of theology. He disliked being called Barthian, for the work of theology was the work of the entire church, not one person nor of a few outstanding people. In his *Letters: 1961–1968*, he mentions a number of times his hope that younger people will take up the task of writing Christian theology. Barth in no manner intended his theology to be definitive, or final, or normal, but to be the attempt of one man who gave his whole life to the task of theology to state what he thinks the church ought to be preaching.

In my own reading of Barth, certain problems in his theology kept cropping up, at least in the sense that I saw things differently from the way he did. The following is a brief summary of some of those issues:

Supralapsarianism

Calvinists in former years debated whether God elected people as people prior to their being viewed as sinners, or whether they were elected as sinners. Those who believed God elected people as people are called *supralapsarians*. Those who believe that God elected persons as sinners are called *sublapsarians*. Benjamin Warfield argued that standard Calvinism was sublapsarian.

It is my impression that Barth's theology is a special kind of supralapsarianism. He gives the impression of teaching that God created the whole human race to be saved. He seems to argue, like Origen, that since all people were lost in Adam they shall be saved in Christ. If God created the whole human race to be saved, then he elected them as people prior to sin and not as sinners. This position is a form of supralapsarianism. And I think Warfield's point stands that the whole presumption of the Christian Gospel is that first of all the elect person is reckoned as a sinner.

On one occasion, Barth said that a young American student at Heidelberg understood the center of his theology. That young American student was Robert W. Jenson, who published his doctoral dissertation in a revised form as *Alpha and Omega: A Study in the Theology of Karl Barth.* Jenson does not use the term *supralapsarian.* He does indicate that Barth does not view the typical version of things as the correct one; namely, that after humanity was created and sinned, God willed to rescue humanity by the incarnation. From the very beginning of God's decrees, God wills to be our redeemer through the incarnation. This position means, as I have said, that we are elected as people, not as sinners. But Barth is so thorough on this point he even could be called a *super-supralapsarian.*

The truth of the matter is that at this point Barth differs most radically from traditional orthodox and evangelical theology, not in the doctrines of revelation and inspiration. Traditional theology has followed the path of Anselm and has seen the incarnation and cross as a remedy for sin *after sin occurred.* Barth unifies creation and redemption in Christology ("redemption is the inner meaning of creation; creation is the external presupposition of redemption"), and hence Christ and the fullness of his work was the first thought of God, not an afterthought.

Biblical Criticism

Barth presumes that he has made peace with biblical criticism and theology by giving each such a job description so that there is no conflict. He does admit that he disagrees with certain practitioners of biblical criticism because they step over the job description, but in his method there is harmony between theology and biblical criticism. Therefore he does not (like the evangelicals) have to perpetually be on the attack against biblical criticism, nor does he (like those of liberal Christianity) have to capitulate to all that passes in the name of criticism. If he has achieved such a peace, it is a great thing.

However, biblical criticism is becoming more critical and more skeptical. We now have "sociological biblical criticism," "scientific-historical biblical criticism," and "economic"—even Marxist—"biblical criticism." This more radical biblical criticism could pull Barth's synthesis apart. It is even possible that there will be a division among biblical scholars themselves about the future character of biblical criticism. Certainly the gap between evangelical scholars and the newer type of criticism is growing very large.

Universalism

From Barth's *Letters: 1961-1968*, it is evident that he tired of being badgered about universalism. He asked his questioners to first read the *Church Dogmatics* and then ask questions. I have attempted to give Barth the benefit of the doubt in my discussion of his universalism. But the question will not go away. As one wag put it, Christianity isn't important unless "somebody around here can get dammed." Or as T. S. Eliot put it, if we eliminate the doctrine of final judgment we convert God into Santa Claus—"Everybody shall get toys and be glad." Barth has not taught universalism in so many words and cannot be charged formally with teaching it. But the very fact that the charge persists indicates that Barth shows a strong bent toward the doctrine. And Brunner voices a suspicion that in some instances Barth has stepped across the line.

Metaphysics

Barth attempted to write his theology in total independence from any philosophy (although as a sinner he knew he could not really do so). On the other hand, he confesses that every human being has some sort of philosophical system by which to organize experiences and life. Is Barth's theology, then, free from metaphysics?

Of course, he denied repeatedly that Christianity was involved in world views. Revelation did not teach a world view. It is therefore free from metaphysics.

I am sure the philosophical community would be very skeptical of the claim that a work of thirteen huge volumes was written free from some major metaphysical assumptions. Perhaps Barth thinks that by definition a theological assumption is not a metaphysical one, whereas philosophers would not make that distinction. Perhaps even the notion that there are metaphysical statements and theological nonmetaphysical statements is itself a metaphysical claim. And perhaps the Swedish critics of Barth are right that in a most comprehensive definition of existentialism (limiting all remarks to purely statements about humanity and its relationships) Barth's theology is existentialist.

Schleiermacher

As much as Barth disagreed with Schleiermacher's theology, he nevertheless expects to see him in heaven.[1] There are some very severe passages in the New Testament about those who confuse the Gospel (Galatians 1:6–9) and those who deny the incarnation (I John 2:22–23, 4:1–6). Has Barth heard the Word of God in these texts? A universalism of the salvation of theologians would be an odd piece of Christian theology.

Barth could show theological wrath! He commented that one of the things that came with growing older was an increasing patience with other views. He is famous for his angry reply to Brunner's program in theology, and he claimed he fought Bultmann with all the energy of his scholarship. Maybe God thinks of Schleiermacher the same way Barth felt about Brunner when Barth issued his wrathful *no!*

Surely in the last day some theologians will be found among the goats. If, as Barth himself said, Schleiermacher's God cannot show mercy, maybe Schleiermacher is to be found among the goats ("By definition, the God of Schleiermacher cannot show mercy").[2]

Overburdened Christology

Whether Barth is a Christomonist or Christocentrist largely depends on the definition one gives those terms. But there is no question about the fact that Barth wishes to interpret every doctrine from a Christological perspective, beginning with creation. Barth takes certain Christological texts in the New Testament with a radical thoroughness unprecedented in the history of theology. These texts are exploited to their fullest. No doubt previous theologians underestimated the implications of these texts. My impression is that Barth overloads his theology with Christology. As great a Christocentric and Christological book that the New Testament is, I never get the impression that it loads as much theological freight on Christology as Barth does.

Continental

Although Barth had a magnificent control of historical theology, he nonetheless writes very much as a German-Swiss continental. Barth himself confesses that he is too much a child of the nineteenth century.[3] Barth's reference to non-German language books is very scarce. The English literature on both sides of the ocean is ignored. There is a German maxim that if there is a good book on a subject in English, there is also one in German and perhaps better, so why read the English one? If Barth did not believe that maxim, he at least practiced it.

It is true that Barth had a stream of students coming to his lectures from all over the world and that he did participate in interchurch, interfaith conferences. However, if he had used a good sampling of works in the English language, he would have greatly increased his hearing in the English-speaking world. As it is, it takes considerable effort for an American student to make him- or herself familiar with the continental scene in order to properly interpret Barth.

Rewriting

Cornelius Van Til has written a small library of criticism of Barth. His major apprehension is that in recasting the older doctrines Barth has actually destroyed them. This charge is serious and important regardless of the criticism that has been leveled against the way van Til has written against Barth. This is the point of my major apprehension regarding Barth's theology.

Has he brilliantly restated the historic Christian faith so as to bring it fully into the twentieth century, or has he in the process of rewriting it shoved it off base? Are his novel interpretations of humanity, sin, and unbelief really remarkable new Scriptural insights, or are they serious deviations? I have given Barth the best interpretation. The reassessment of Barth cannot take place until tempers cool and prejudices dissipate. Then he may be studied for what he truly wrote. And in that process of sustained study it will be determined whether Barth has given a brilliant restatement of the historic Christian faith for the twentieth century or whether he was an eccentric genius with more eccentricity than genius.

In that I have said so much about Karl Barth and his theology in an approving way, one could conclude that I have been blinded by him. The purpose of this appendix is to show that I have attempted to be as objective about Barth as I am approving. And if I have challenged the older evangelical paradigm in theology, I am not offering a new one as if it were free from all internal problems.

Notes

1. Karl Barth, *Letters: 1961–1968,* trans. Goeffrey Bromiley (Grand Rapids, Mich.: Eerdmans, 1981), p. 288.
2. Karl Barth, *Evangelical Theology: An Introduction,* trans. Grover Foley (New York: Holt, Rinehart & Winston, 1963), p. 10.
3. Barth, *Letters: 1961–1968,* p. 101.

Lewis Sperry Chafer and Karl Barth

Lewis Sperry Chafer's *Systematic Theology* (8 vols.) is a standard text in a number of evangelical and fundamentalist schools. It is heralded as the fullest text of systematic theology that we have now in print for evangelicals. It claims to be unabridged, premillennial, and dispensational. It is, then, a paradigm for evangelical and fundamentalist theology. No doubt in comparing the two men is somewhat like comparing apples and oranges. They had different careers, taught in very different educational institutions, faced some different problems, and served different people. However, for what it is worth, as the two theologians stand for two different paradigms, let us make a modest comparison.

Education

Chafer spent three years at Oberlin College and then left to teach in a school for boys that D. L. Moody had founded. That was the sum total of Chafer's formal education.

Barth studied in the universities of Bern, Marburg, Berlin, and Tübingen. He studied under such men as Adolph von Harnack, Reinhold Seeberg, Julius Kaftan, Herman Gunkel, Theodor Häring, Wilhelm Herrmann, Johannes Weiss, and

Adolph Jülicher. In philosophy, he studied under the famous neo-Kantians Hermann Cohen and Paul Natorp. In addition, Barth eventually was honored with eleven doctorates from substantial universities and collected a number of prizes and awards.

C. F. Lincoln cites Chafer himself as saying, "The very fact that I did not study a prescribed course in theology made it possible for me to approach the subject with an unprejudiced mind to be concerned only with what the Bible actually teaches."[1] In his memorial to Chafer, Lincoln puts it in his own words: "He was also unhampered by the molding influence of any specific denominational, doctrinal or organizational bias, and was free to search the Scriptures themselves for the formulation of curriculum and doctrines."[2]

Linguistic Preparation

Having had no formal theological education, Chafer also had no linguistic training. It is apparent from his *Systematic Theology* that he is always working with secondary sources, whether in the biblical languages or theological literature.

Having gone through the typical Swiss gymnasium (a sort of high school in Germany and Switzerland to prepare students for university), Barth was taught Latin, Greek, and French. When he came to the Scripture, he worked with both the Hebrew and Greek Testaments, and when he cites the church fathers he cites the original Greek or Latin. In addition, he could speak the modern languages of Swiss German, German, English, French, and Italian, and complained of his poor ability in Dutch.

Philosophy

In reading Chafer's theology, it is apparent that he is not at home at all in philosophy. He makes rare references to philosophers, and in most cases Chafer is citing some other source and not the philosopher directly.

Barth learned philosophy from Cohen and Natorp. His writings show that he is totally competent in philosophy, having written technical interpretations of such philosophers as Kant, Hegel, Heidegger, Jaspers, and Sartre. Wherever he does get into philosophical territory, he handles the matters with competence. Naturally he knew well the philosophy of Anselm and Thomas Aquinas. As previously mentioned, he had certain limitations, being oriented so much to continental studies. Hence he does not interact with the English and American traditions in philosophy.

Historical Theology

Chafer's coverage of historical theology is minimal. Although he cites Augustine, Calvin, Edwards, and others, he does so almost uniformly from a secondary source. Judging from his published theology, he had rarely read the original works of the great theologians.

Barth's coverage of historical theology is monumental. Furthermore, he always cites them in their original language. It is generally conceded that if Barth had chosen to specialize in historical theology he would have written the most definitive book in the history of theology. As the *Church Dogmatics* now stands, its many sections of historical theology make the reading of the text valuable alone for that reason. If one has no use for Barth's theology, there is still great worth in reading it for historical theology.

Citation of Scripture

Chafer's citation of Scripture is modest. There are not more than 800 references in the index.

Barth's citation of Scripture is the greatest in the history of theology—15,000. Furthermore, there are 2,000 long and short exegetical sections in the *Church Dogmatics*, showing Barth's intense occupation with the text of Scripture. And in addition to that are all the concept concordances of Scriptural texts scattered throughout the *Church Dogmatics*. Even master's theses and doctoral dissertations on Barth never give the proper impression of Barth's vast knowledge of Holy Scripture, his incessant citing of it, and the numerous exegetical inserts.

Notes

1. C. F. Lincoln, "Biographical Sketch of the Author," in Lewis Sperry Chafer, *Systematic Theology*, vol. 8 (Dallas: Dallas Seminary Press, 1948), pp. 5–6.
2. C. F. Lincoln, "Lewis Sperry Chafer," *Bibliotheca Sacra* 109 (1952), p. 337.

Bibliography

By Barth

Anselm: Fides Quaerens Intellectum. Translated by Ian Roberts. Richmond: John Knox Press, 1960.

Die Botschaft von der freien Gnaden Gottes: Theologische Studien, Heft 23. Zollikon–Zürich: Evangelischer Verlag, 1947.

The Christian Life. Edited and translated by Goeffrey Bromiley. Grand Rapids: Wm. B. Eerdmans, 1981.

Church Dogmatics. (13 vols.) Edited and translated by Goeffrey Bromiley, F. F. Bruce, et al. Edinburgh: T. & T. Clark, 1936–1969.

The Epistle to the Romans. Translated by Edwyn C. Hoskyns. Oxford: Oxford University Press, 1932.

Evangelical Theology, records 3231–3237. Waco: Word Records, 1962.

Evangelical Theology: An Introduction. Translated by Grover Foley. New York: Holt Rinehart and Winston, 1963.

Faith of the Church. Translated by Gabriel Vahanian. New York: Living Age Books, 1958.

Fragments Grave and Gay. Translated by Eric Mosbacher. London: Collins, 1971.

Das Geschenk der Freiheit: Theologische Studien, Heft 39. Zollikon–Zürich: Evangelischer Verlag, 1953.

Humanismus: Theologische Studien, Heft 28. Zollikon–Zürich: Evangelischer Verlag, 1949.

The Humanity of God. Translated by J. N. Thomas and T. Weiser. Richmond: John Knox Press, 1960.

"Liberal Theology: Some Alternatives." Translated by L. A. Garrard. In *The Hibbert Journal* 59 (April 1961), pp. 213–219.

Natural Theology (with Emil Brunner). Translated by P. Fraenkel. London: Goeffrey Bles, 1946.

"Philosophie und Theologie." In *Philosophie und Geschichtliche Existenz: Festchrift für Heinrich Barth,* edited by G. Huber, pp. 93–106. Basel: Helbing und Lichtenhahn, 1969.

Protestant Theology in the Nineteenth Century. Translated by B. Cozens and H. H. Hartwell. Valley Forge: Judson Press, 1968.

"Rudolph Bultmann—An Attempt to Understand Him." In *Kerygma and Myth,* edited by Hans-Werner Bartsch, translated by R. H. Fuller, pp. 83–132. London: SPCK, 1962.

A Shorter Commentary on Romans. Translated by D. H. Van Daalen. Richmond: John Knox Press, 1959.

Die Theologie Schleiermachers. Zürich: Theologischer Verlag, 1978.

Die Wirklichkeit des Neuen Menschen: Theologische Studien, Heft 27. Zollikon-Zürich: Evangelischer Verlag, 1950.

The Word of God and the Word of Man. Translated by Douglas Horton. New York: Harper Torchbook edition, 1957.

Interviews and Seminars. These occurred in the academic year of 1957–1958 (Winter and Summer semesters). The interviews took place in Barth's private residence in Basel, Switzerland. The seminars were the English-speaking seminars held in a local restaurant.

About Barth

Babbitt, Irving. *Democracy and Leadership.* Boston: Houghton Mifflin, 1924.

Baillie, John. "Some Reflections on the Changing Theological Scene." *Union Quarterly Seminary Review* 12 (November 1956), pp. 3–9.

Barr, James. *Fundamentalism.* Philadelphia: Westminister Press, 1977.

Barth, Marcus. "Response." *Union Seminary Quarterly Review* 28 (Fall 1972), pp. 53–54.

Baumann, Urs. *Erbsünde? Ihr traditionelles Verständnis in der Krise heutiger Theologie.* Freiburg: Herder, 1970.

Berkouwer, Gerrit. *The Return of Christ.* Edited by Marvin J. Van Elderen; translated by James Van Osterom. Grand Rapids: Wm. B. Eerdmans, 1972.

——— . *The Triumph of Grace in the Theology of Karl Barth.* Translated by Harry R. Boer. Grand Rapids: Wm. B. Eerdmans, 1956.

Biéler, André. *The Social Humanism of Calvin.* Translated by Paul T. Fuhrmann. Richmond: John Knox Press, 1964

Blackstone, William. *Jesus Is Coming.* New York: Fleming H. Revell, 1908.

Bloesch, Donald. *Jesus Is Victor: Karl Barth's Doctrine of Salvation.* Nashville: Abingdon, 1976.

Boice, James Montogomery, ed. *The Foundation of Biblical Authority.* Grand Rapids: Zondervan, 1978.

Bolich, Gregory. *Karl Barth and Evangelicalism.* Downers Grove: InterVarsity Press, 1980.

Bossuet, Jacques-Bénigne. *Discours sur l' histoire universel.* Paris, 1681.

Bromiley, Goeffrey. *Introduction to the Theology of Karl Barth.* Grand Rapids: Wm. B. Eerdmans, 1979.

Bühlmann, Albert. *The Search for God.* Maryknoll, N.Y.: Orbis Books, 1980.

Busch, Eberhard. *Karl Barth: His Life from Letters and Autobiographical Texts.* Translated by John Bowden. Philadelphia: Fortress Press, 1976.

Butterfield, Herbert. *Man on His Past: The Study of the History of Historical Scholarship.* Cambridge: Cambridge University Press, 1969.

Calvin, John. *Institutes of the Christian Religion,* Vol. I. Translated by Ford Lewis Battles. Philadelphia: Westminster Press, 1960.

Cassirer, Ernst. *The Philosophy of the Enlightenment.* Translated by Fritz C. A. Koelln and James F. Pettegrove. Boston: Beacon Press, 1951.

Chafer, Lewis Sperry. *Sperry Theology.* 8 vols. Dallas: Dallas Seminary Press, 1947.

Clark, Gordon. *Historiography Secular and Religious.* Nutley, N.J.: Craig Press, 1971.

——— . *Karl Barth's Theological Method.* Philipsburg, N.J.: Presbyterian and Reformed Publishing Co., 1963.

Darwin, Charles. *The Origin of Species.* New York: New American Library, Mentor Books, 1958 [1859].

Dickerman, David L., ed. *Karl Barth and the Future of Theology.* New Haven: Yale Divinity School Association, 1969.

Dollar, George W. *A History of Fundamentalism in America.* Greenville, N.C.: Bob Jones University Press, 1973.

Dostoyevkski, Fedor. *The Brothers Karamazov.* 2 vols. Baltimore: Penguin Books, 1958.

Dumas, André. "Theologie et humanisme." In *Hommage et Reconnaissance* [de Karl Barth], edited by Jean–Jacques von Allmen, pp. 195–207. Neuchatel: Delachaux et Niestlé, 1946.

Dunn, James D. G. *Christology in the Making.* Philadelphia: Westminster Press, 1980.

——— . *Unity and Diversity in the New Testament.* Philadelphia: Westminster Press, 1977.

Ebeling, Gerhard. *Word and Faith.* Translated by James W. Leitch. Philadelphia: Fortress Press, 1963.

Eliot, T. S. *Selected Essays.* New edition. New York: Harcourt, Brace and Co., 1950.

Ellis, Ieun. *Seven Against Christ: A Study in 'Essays and Reviews.'* Leiden: E. J. Brill, 1980.

Ferm, Deane William. *Contemporary American Theologies.* New York: Seabury Press, 1981.

Forsyth, Peter Taylor. *The Principle of Authority.* London: Hodder and Stoughton, 1912.

Fürst, Walther. "Karl Barths Predigt Lehre." In *Antwort: Karl Barth zum Siebzigsten Gebürtstag am 10 Mai 1956,* edited by Ernst Wolf, Ch. von Kirschbaum, and Rudolph Frey, pp. 137–147. Zollikon–Zürich: Evangelischer Verlag, 1956.

Gay, Peter. *The Enlightenment: An Interpretation.* New York: Knopf, 1967

Geisler, Norman, ed. *Inerrancy.* Grand Rapids: Zondervan, 1979.

Godsey, John. *Karl Barth's Table Talk.* Richmond: John Knox, 1962.

Grousset, Réne, et al. *Pour un nouvel humanisme: Rencontres Genève,* 1949. Neuchatel: Éditions de la Baconniere, 1949.

Hazard, Paul. *The European Mind: 1680–1715.* Translated by J. Lewis May. Cleveland: World Publishing Co., 1935.

——— . *European Thought in the Eighteenth Century.* Translated by J. Lewis May. Cleveland: World Publishing Co., 1946.

Henry, Carl F. H. *God, Revelation and Authority*. 4 vols. Waco: Word, 1976–1979.

Highet, Gilbert. *The Classical Tradition*. New York: Oxford University Press, 1957.

Hodge, Charles. *Systematic Theology*, Vol. I, New York: Scribner, Armstrong and Co., 1873.

Hughes, Philip Edgcumbe. *Interpreting Prophecy*. Grand Rapids: Wm. B. Eerdmans, 1976.

Jensen, Robert. *Alpha and Omega: A Study in the Theology of Karl Barth*. New York: Nelson, 1963.

Kant, Immanuel. *The Critique of Judgment*. Translated by James Creed Meredith. Oxford: Clarendon Press, 1952.

———. *The Critique of Practical Reason*. Translated by Lewis White Beck. Chicago: University of Chicago Press, 1949.

———. *The Critique of Pure Reason*. Translated by Norman Kemp Smith. New York: Humanities Press, 1950.

Kliever, Lonnie. *The Shattered Spectrum*. Atlanta: John Knox Press, 1981.

Kraus, Hans-Joachim. "Das Problem der Heilsgeschichte in der 'Kirklich Dogmatik.'" In *Antwort: Karl Barth zum Siebzigsten Gebürtstag am 10 Mai 1956*, edited by Ernst Wolf, Ch. von Kirschbaum, and Rudolph Frey, pp. 69–83. Zollikon-Zürich: Evangelischer Verlag, 1956.

Küng, Hans. *Does God Exist?* Translated by Edward Quinn. Garden City: Doubleday, 1980.

Kuyper, Abraham. *Principles of Sacred Theology*. Translated by J. Hendrik De Vries. Grand Rapids: Wm. B. Eerdmans, 1954.

Larkin, Clarence. *Dispensational Truth*. Third ed. Philadelphia: Rev. Clarence Larkin Est., 1920.

Lawrence, Jerome, and Lee, Robert E. *Inherit the Wind*. New York: Bantam, 1960.

Lessing, Gotthold Ephraim. *Nathan the Wise*. Translated by Bayard Quincy Morgan. New York: Frederick Ungar, 1972.

Lewis, C. S., "The Funeral of a Great Myth." In *Christian Reflections*. Grand Rapids: Wm. B. Eerdmans, 1967.

———. *The Great Divorce*. New York: Macmillan, 1946.

———. "Modern Theology and Biblical Criticism." In *Christian Reflections*, edited by Walter Hooper, pp. 152–166. Grand Rapids: Wm. B. Eerdmans, 1967.

Lincoln, C. F. "Biographical Sketch of the Author." In Lewis Sperry Chafer, *Systematic Theology*, vol. 8, pp. 3–6. 8 vols. Dallas: Dallas Seminary Press, 1948.

———. "Lewis Sperry Chafer." *Bibliotheca Sacra* 109 (1952), p. 337.

Lindsell, Harold. *The Battle for the Bible*. Grand Rapids: Zondervan, 1976.

Lindsey, Hal. *The Late Great Planet Earth*. Grand Rapids: Zondervan, 1970.

Luther, Martin. *The Bondage of the Will*. Translated by J. I. Packer and C. R. Johnston. Westwood, N.J.: Felming H. Revell, 1957.

McClelland, Joseph C. "Philosophy and Theology—A Family Affair (Karl and Heinrich Barth)." In *Footnotes to a Theology: Karl Barth Colloquium of 1972*, edited by Martin Rumscheidt, pp. 30–52. The Corporation for the Publication of Academic Studies in Religion in Canada, 1974.

McIntyre, John. *St. Anselm and His Critics*. Edinburgh: T. & T. Clark, 1954.

Marsden, George, and Roberts, Frank, ed. *A Christian View of History?* Grand Rapids: Wm. B. Eerdmans, 1975.

May, Henry F. *The Enlightenment in America.* New York: Oxford University Press, 1976.

Mayer, Milton; Allen, Steve; and Fadiman, Clifton. "Three Views of Humor." *The Center Magazine* 4 (Jan./Feb. 1971), pp. 16–22.

Mehl, Roger. *La Condition du Philosophe Chrètien.* Neuchatel: Delachaux et Niestlé, 1947.

Montgomery, John Warwick, ed. *God's Inerrant Word.* Minneapolis: Bethany Fellowship, 1974.

Newman, John Henry. *On the Scope and Nature of University Education.* London: J. E. Dent and Sons, 1915.

Niebuhr, Reinhold. *The Nature and Destiny of Man.* New York: Charles Scribner's Sons, 1948.

Niebuhr, Richard R. *Schleiermacher on Christ and Religion.* New York: Charles Scribner's Sons, 1964.

Ogletree, Thomas. *Christian Faith and History: A Critical Comparison of Ernest Troeltsch and Karl Barth.* New York: Abingdon Press, 1965.

Porter, Roy, and Teich, Mikulaš, eds, *The Enlightenment in National Context.* Cambridge: Cambridge University Press, 1981.

Provence, Edward Thomas. "The Hermeneutics of Karl Barth." Ph.D. dissertation. Fuller Theological Seminary, 1980.

Randall, John Herman, Jr. *The Making of the Modern Mind.* Rev. edition. Boston: Houghton Mifflin, 1940.

Rausch, David A. *Zionism Within Early American Fundamentalism: 1878–1918. Texts and Studies in Religion.* New York: Edward Nellen Press, 1979.

Redeker, Martin. *Schleiermacher: Life and Thought.* Translated by John Wallhauser. Philadelphia: Fortress Press, 1973.

Renckens, Henricus. *Israel's Concept of the Beginnings: The Theology of Genesis 1– 3.* Translated by Charles Napier. New York: Herder and Herder, 1964.

Richardson, Alan. *History Sacred and Profane.* London: SCM Press, 1964.

Ritschl, Dietrich. *A Theology of Proclamation.* Richmond: John Knox Press, 1960.

Robinson, James, M., ed. *The Beginnings of Dialectical Theology,* Vol. I. Translated by Keith R. Crim and Louis De Grazia. Richmond: John Knox Press, 1968.

Rozeboom, John A. "Preaching in the Theology of Karl Barth: The Question of Its Urgency and Significance." Ph.D. dissertation. Fuller Theological Seminary, 1974.

Runia, Klaas. *Karl Barth's Doctrine of Holy Scripture.* Grand Rapids: Wm. B. Eerdmans, 1962.

Sartre, Jean-Paul. *Existentialism.* Translated by Bernard Frechtman. New York: Philosophical Library, 1947.

Sauter, Gerhard. *Zukunft and Verheissung.* Zurich: Zwingli Verlag, 1965.

Sayers, Dorothy L. *Creed or Chaos?* London: The Religious Book Club, 1947.

Schaeffer, Francis. *Genesis in Space and Time.* Downers Grove: InterVarsity Press, 1972.

Schleiermacher, Friedrich. *The Christian Faith.* Translated by H. R. Mackintosh and James Stewart. Edinburgh: T. & T. Clark, 1928.

——— . *On Religion: Speeches to Its Cultured Despisers.* Translated by John Oman.

New York: Harper Torch Book edition, 1958 [1893].

Schmithals, Walter. *The Apocalyptic Movement.* Translated by John E. Steeley. Nashville: Abingdon Press, 1975.

Schwarz, Hans. *On the Way to the Future.* Minneapolis: Augsburg Publishing House, 1972.

Scofield, Cyrus I. *Rightly Dividing the Word of Truth.* New York: Fleming H. Revell, 1907.

——— . *The Scofield Reference Bible.* New and Improved edition. London: Oxford University Press, 1917.

——— . *The Seven Dispensations.* St Paul: Asher Publishing Company, n.d.

Senf, Christof. *Wahrhaftigkeit und Wahrheit: Die Theologie zwischen Orthodoxie und Aufkärung.* Tübingen: Paul Mohr, 1956.

Smith, John E. "The Significance of Karl Barth's Thought on the Relation Between Theology and Philosophy." *Union Seminary Quarterly Review* 28 (Fall 1972) pp.15–30. Robert W. Jenson. "Response," pp. 31–36.

Solzhenitsyn, Aleksandr. *The Gulag Archipelago.* 2 vols. Translated by Thomas P. Whitney. New York: Harper & Row, 1973–74.

Sykes, S. W., ed. *Karl Barth—Studies of His Theological Method.* Oxford: Clarendon Press, 1979.

Temple, Frederick, et al. *Essays and Reviews.* London: Parker, 1860.

Thielicke, Helmut. *The Evangelical Faith, Vol 1.* Translated by Goeffrey Bromiley. Grand Rapids: Wm. B. Eerdmans, 1974.

——— . *How Modern Should Theology Be?* Translated by A. George Anderson. Philadelphia: Fortress Press, 1969.

Thornton, Lionel. *Revelation and the Modern World.* London: Dacre Press, 1950.

Thurneysen, Eduard. "Die Anfänge." In *Antwort: Karl Barth zum Siebzigsten Gebürtstag am 10 Mai 1956,* edited by Ernst Wolf, Ch. von Kirschbaum, and Rudolph Frey. Zollikon-Zürich: Evangelischer Verlag, 1956.

Tillich, Paul. *A History of Christian Thought.* London: SCM Press, 1968.

——— . *Perspectives in 19th and 20th Century Theology.* New York: Harper & Row, 1967.

Torrance, Thomas. *Karl Barth: An Introduction to His early Theology: 1920–1931.* London: SCM Press, 1962.

——— . *Theological Science.* New York: Oxford University Press, 1969.

Traub, Hellmutt. "Theologie und Verkündigen." In *Antwort: Karl Barth zum Siebzigsten Gebürtstag am 10 Mai 1956,* edited by Ernst Wolf. Ch. von Kirschbaum, and Rudolph Frey. Zollikon-Zürich: Evangelischer Verlag, 1956.

Van Til, Cornelius. *Karl Barth and Evangelicalism.* Philadelphia: Presbyterian and Reformed Publishing Co., 1964.

——— . *The New Modernism.* Philipsburg, N.J. : Presbyterian and Reformed Publishing Co., 1973.

——— . *The Sovereignty of Grace: An Appraisal of G. C. Berkouwer's View of Dordt.* Philadelphia: Presbyterian and Reformed Publishing Co., 1969.

Vawter, Bruce. *Inspiration.* Philadelphia: Westminster Press, 1973.

Vogel, Heinrich. *Gott in Christo.* 2nd ed. Berlin: Lettner Verlag, 1952.

——— . "Der lachende Barth." In *Antwort: Karl Barth zum Siebzigsten Gebürtstag am 10 Mai 1956,* edited by Ernst Wolf, Ch. von Kirschbaum, and Rudolph Frey. Zollikon-Zürich: Evangelischer Verlag, 1956.

Warfield, Benjamin. *The Plan of Salvation*. Grand Rapids: Wm. B. Eerdmans, 1965.

Warnock, Mary. *Ethics Since 1900*. London: Oxford University Press, 1960.

Wharton, James A. "Karl Barth as Exegete in His Influence on Biblical Interpretation." *Union Seminary Quarterly Review* 28 (Fall 1972) pp. 5–14.

Whitehouse, W. A. *Creation, Science and Theology: Essays in Response to Karl Barth*. Grand Rapids: Wm. B. Eerdmans, 1981.

Wolf, Ernst; von Kirschbaum, Ch.; and Frey, Rudolph, eds. *Antwort: Karl Barth zum Siebzigsten Gebürtstag am 10 Mai 1956*. Zollikon-Zürich: Evangelischer Verlag, 1956.

Yao, Leoncio. "Barth's Dynamic Concept of the Freedom of Man." Th.M. thesis, Fuller Theological Seminary, 1966.

Yu Carver Tatsum. "Barth's Theological Method and the Problem of Historicity." Th. M. thesis, Fuller Theological Seminary, 1976.

Encyclopedia Articles

Anz, Wilhelm. "Aufklärung." *Religion in Geschichte und Gegenwart*, I:703–730.

Berlin, Isaiah. "Counter-Enlightenment." *Dictionary of the History of Ideas*. II:100–112.

Fahlbusch, Erwin, und Schümmer, Franz. "Aufklärung." *Evangelisches Kirchen Lexikon*, I:248–253.

Geense, Adriaan. "Freiheit." *Taschenlexikon: Religion und Theologie*, A-G: 289–291.

Hecker, Conrad. "Humanism." *Sacramentum Mundi*, 3:74–78.

Hoffmann-Axtheim, Diether. "Aufklärung." *Taschenlexikon: Religion und Theologie*, A-G: 70–75.

Holmes, Arthur F. "Christian Philosphy." *Encyclopaedia Britannica* (15), IV:555–562.

"Humanism." *Encyclopaedia Britannica* (15), V:199.

Jüngel, Eberhard. "Karl Barth." *Theologische Realenzyklopädie*. V:251-268.

Koestler, Arthur. "Humor and Wit." *Encyclopaedia Britannica* (15), IX:5–11.

Lorenzmeier, Theodor. "Predigt." *Taschenlexikon: Religion und Theologie*, L-R: 188–192.

Palsson, Herman. "Saga." *Encyclopaedia Britannica* (15), XVI:145–157.

Pappe, Hellmut O. "Enlightenment." *Dictionary of the History of Ideas*, II:89-100.

Philipp, Wolfgang. "Neologie." *Evangelisches Kirchen Lexikon*, II:1541–1544.

Raab, Heribert. "Enlightenment." *Sacramentum Mundi*, II:230-232.

Troeltsch, Ernst. "The Enlightenment." *The New Schaff-Herzog Encyclopedia of Religious Knowledge*, IV:141–147.

"Vincentian Canon." *The Oxford Dictionary of the Christian Church* (second ed.), p. 1443.

Index